T0150232

Beyond the Briar Patch

Beyond the Briar Patch

Affrilachian Tales, Food and Folklore

Lyn Ford

Parkhurst Brothers Publishers

MARION, MICHIGAN

www.parkhurstbrothers.com

Parkhurst Brothers books are distributed to the trade through the Chicago Distribution Center, and may be ordered through Ingram Book Company, Baker & Taylor, Follett Library Resources and other book industry wholesalers. To order from Chicago Distribution Center, phone 1-800-621-2736 or send a fax to 800-621-8476. Copies of this and other Parkhurst Brothers Inc., Publishers titles are available to organizations and corporations for purchase in quantity by contacting Special Sales Department at our home office location, listed on our web site. Manuscript submission guidelines for this publishing company are available at our web site.

Printed in the United States on America
The quality paper on which this book is printed was milled in the U.S.A.
First Edition, 2014
2014 2015 2016 2017 2018   12 11 10 9 8 7 6 5 4 3 2 1
Library of Congress Cataloging-in-Publication Data

Ford, Lyn, 1951- author.
  Beyond the briar patch : Affrilachian folktales, food and folklore / Lyn Ford. -- First Edition.
      pages cm
  Summary: «Lyn Ford, an African-American storyteller, honored by her peers nationally, retells traditional stories and folkways from her cultural heritage»-- Provided by publisher.
  ISBN 978-1-62491-025-8 (paperback) -- ISBN 978-1-62491-026-5 (ebk.)
  1. African Americans--Appalachian Region--Folklore. 2. African Americans-- Appalachian Region--Social life and customs. 3. Tales--Appalachian Region. 4. Ford, Lyn, 1951---Childhood and youth. 5. Appalachian Region--Social life and customs. I. Title.
  GR111.A47F673 2014
  398.2089›96073--dc23
                        2014017355

This book is printed on archival-quality paper that meets the requirements of the American National Standard for Information Sciences, Permanence of Paper, Printed Library Materials, ANSI Z39.48-043-2

ISBN: Trade Paperback   978162491-025-8
ISBN: e-book   978162491-026-5

Cover photograph, cover and interior design by   Linda D. Parkhurst, Ph.D.
Acquired for Parkhurst Brothers Publishers and
edited by: Ted Parkhurst
Proofread by   Bill and Barbara Paddack
102014

Dedicated with fondness to the memory of
Great-Grandma Essie Arkward
🙿 I wish you had told me *your* story 🙿

and
also with tremendous love for
Bruce
whose story is so much a part of mine.

"Listen to my story, and ev'rything'll come out true ... "
Lyrics from the song *Blue Blues*
sung by Bessie Smith (1894–1937), "Empress of the Blues,"
born an Affrilachian in Chattanooga, Tennessee

Acknowledgments
Thank You, Folks!

In the Preface to this book, and the story notes for "Fox and Crow," I mention a wonderful storytelling journey in Kentucky. My driver on that occasion was Shane Barton, program coordinator for the Appalachian Center at the University of Kentucky; he shared funny and heartfelt stories of his large family's gatherings and tale-tellings, and the influence that tradition had on him as he grew up. We talked about how the coal and rail industries impacted on the lives of both our families. I loved listening to his experiences as a project and program coordinator. I watched as he took a picture of a small post office for the Appalachian Kentucky Post Office Project, which is documenting the past and present contributions of post office workers and post offices in Appalachian Kentucky. Wonderful!

Dr. Sasikumar Balasundaram, Postdoctoral Scholar at the UKY Appalachian Center, is mentioned as the storyteller who, by sharing a variant of the tale, sparked a memory of and ignited a fire to tell "Fox and Crow". Thank-you, Sasi!

Meeting us in Pikeville was Stephanie Richards, Pike County's fine arts extension agent for the Cooperative Extension Program. Stephanie had communicated with Shane, and arranged my storytelling visit at Majestic-Knoxville Elementary School, where sixty-three attentive students joyfully participated in a day of Affrilachian folktale interaction. Stephanie spoke of returning to Appalachia from her acting work in Chicago, knowing that was what she was meant to do. She also told me of the Artists Collaborative Theatre where folks in Elkhorn City can enjoy great entertainment all year long, and of the young people in her theater group, students who are willing to give up a tremendous amount of time to learning and sharing drama and theater management skills. I marveled at her energy and efforts, and listened with great admiration to the success stories of Pike County's interest in local arts. Unbelievably great work, Stephanie!

Without the push from my publisher and friend, Ted Parkhurst, I wouldn't have written the first book, or taken a chance on putting together this second one. Thanks, Ted!

If I hadn't enjoyed such wonderful tellers feeding my brain with stories during my childhood, I wouldn't have the material or foundation to do my storytellin' thang today. Thank you to the ancestors and elders mentioned in the Preface, especially my parents, Edward Maclin Cooper and Jean E. Arkward Cooper Matthews, who told and read stories to us in the first and foremost years, and Pop-Pops, Byard Wilmer Arkward, who made the telling of a story seem as easy as breathing. And thank you to my stepfather, the late James M. Matthews, for saying those words, "Go for it, Sissy!" when I said I wanted to try to become a full-time storyteller. He was one of my cheerleaders.

I love my children, Benjamin, Brandon, and Bonnie, and am grateful to them for pushing me into a storytelling career. They volunteered me to tell our traditional stories in their schools many, many years ago, and they have always believed in their mama. I love my husband, Bruce, and am more than grateful for his patience with my mutterings as I work, and for his blindness to my filing system—a small *mountain range* of papers wherever I'm working—as well as for his partnership as my "roadie," and for his unconditional love.

And, as always and forever, thanks to the man who made the word "the word." Frank X. Walker, you gave this storyteller and her people a name for who we proudly are, Affrilachian!

Contents

Preface

The Rabbit In That Briar Patch?

A briar patch is a thicket of plants or bushes, dense, tangled, and thorny. Its place in literature and the arts has grown from the prickly patch Brer Rabbit claims as the place where he was "bred and born" to a dangerous nebula in the *Star Trek* movies universe.[1]

In Groveport, Ohio, Briar Patch Ranch for Kids is a farm/ranching program for at-risk students, in which youth are introduced to hands-on experiences that help them overcome past difficulties with everything from being bullied to being the bully, from severe lack of self-discipline to severe depression, from living a hard life to hardly living at all. Students as young as eight study with their teachers for half the day, then run the farm during the other half. They tend horses, handle the responsibilities of ranching, including gardening chores, work in the orchards, and merchandise produce. Older students mentor the younger ones. The work is physically hard. Mentally and emotionally, the love is tough. Through it, the students thrive and grow, as Rabbit did in his prickly home.

Bred and born in the briar patch? Yes, some rabbits are born in thickets, and some are thrown there* by mean folks like Brer Bear and Brer Wolf. Besides those born into the thickets, there are others who walk into the thicket, and realize, after a time, that they need to walk out again.

But, for my mother's and grandmother's generations of women, the symbolism of this life went far beyond a thorny place of birth. In some parts of the hills, a "briar patch child" was one who was conceived "on the wrong side of the blanket" and born out of wedlock. Sometimes, that meant conception within an immature but loving relationship. Sometimes, it meant conception through force, without the consent of the woman who would bear this child. Although the plantation social model was not a strong contributor to the socio-economic foundation of the Appalachian region, there were breeding plantations in the Shenandoah Valley of Virginia, and in adjacent areas. Many of the children born into this captivity were sent to cotton and sugar plantations outside the Appalachian hills. My mother says that we are, in part, children of the families of "the Carter plantations"[2] of Virginia. The term "briar patch child" was used to refer to some of us, for we were, in part, the descendants of plantation-owning families intermixing with their captive workers.

The briar patch is a thorny situation, into which many of us have been born or pushed, or in some twisted or tricky way prone to visit it. Many rabbits' lives have begun in such circumstances, and it's a character-building experience, to say the least.

When you have lived in it—or grown through it—and come out of it, you're a different animal. The briar patch takes out the sweet, the cute, the fuzzy bunny part of one who is subjected to its twists. Appearances may be deceiving, but one who has been through the briar patch has felt the thorns of that place, and they have left their marks on the body and on the psyche.

No, do not imagine that a character—or a person—gets through the briar patch without being marked by the thorns. You may do well to think of characters like Manabozho, also known as the Great Hare, the Algonquin trickster god and warrior rabbit. And a quotation about a more familiar character that states, "If you think you can outsmart Brer Rabbit you had better read the tales again."[3] If that's too grand and too mythological an image for you, think Bugs Bunny.

Warner Brothers Cartoons, Inc. writers and illustrators knew Brer Rabbit well; they made his animated descendant the hero of many an adventure, to the chagrin of antagonists like Elmer Fudd and Daffy Duck. But they didn't seem to know how important it was to give the trickster rabbit recognition for his roots. Acknowledging the briar patch in the pedigree of these tales is just as important in our thinking (and our storytelling) today.

In my family, the rabbit was just "Rabbit." "Brer Rabbit" was the character in the Joel Chandler Harris collections of stories gathered from the African ancestors whose "briar patch" was captivity in the Americas. In his publications of the 1800s and early 1900s, Harris gave little recognition to earlier variant tales then still being told in Africa. He did share the names of some of his sources: George Terrell and Old Harbert, Turnwold Plantation captives, during the years of 1862 to 1866 (when Harris' worked for Joseph Addison Turner as a printer's devil for Turner's newspaper, "The Countryman").[4] His attempted use of African-American dialect and creation of the narrator known as Uncle Remus are responsible for the shunning of the tales by many people of African-American heritage. I have seen people cringe at the title "brer," and some of those people were related to me.

In communities where there is little knowledge of the oral traditions and cultural connections behind the tales of Rabbit, some folks look upon Harris' narrator as a stereotype of "the happy slave." They interpret the language of his retellings as a slap in the face to literate and educated persons of color. If the Harris publications are the only versions of these stories that a person, of any "color," hears or reads, he or she has received a limited and skewed perspective of the oral traditions of an American people who are not limited to the region known as "The South," nor to a singular dialect, nor to a single cultural family from the African continent, nor to Harris' versions of the stories.

The briar patch stories told on this side of the Atlantic Ocean arrived with captive Africans. Like their bearers, the stories spread throughout the Americas. Almost immediately, those stories became a folkloric staple of their adopted cultures. Within a few generations, they were widely shared—not only in the southern United States-but also from the coasts of South American through the West Indies into the Florida Keys and all the way up the Appalachian Mountain region into Canada, wherever families of African heritage have made their homes.

The stories are a part of an ancient oral tradition that passes on both knowledge and wisdom. They are rooted in the centuries-old trickster tales of such protagonists as Wakaima the Hare in East Africa, Zomo the Rabbit in West Africa, and Hare or Rabbit by other names in many countries across that continent. The motifs of the so-called "Brer Rabbit" tales are also a part of centuries of stories of Rabbit among the Cherokee and other Algonquin language groups, in the Sanskrit Panchatantra, and the Tio Conejo tales and El Conejito tales of Latin America. So compelling are the African briar patch stories, that they have been accepted into some threads of European-American folk stories transported from coast to coast.

These folktales are recognized today, respected, and loved by most of the world. At the same time, there was a woman in Detroit who feared my telling of such stories at her children's library, because she only knew of the persona of Harris' Uncle Remus and the Disney version of one of the oldest stories in recorded West African folktale and mythology. Until I told from my family's Rabbit stories, and shared a little of the history that I knew about them, this young mother had no idea that her family could find a connection to pre-1800 storytelling from the African Diaspora by listening to these tales.

After the program, with tears in her eyes, the woman introduced me to her children. She said, "This is the first time I ever heard a storyteller. This is the first time I knew where those stories began."

One of my daddy's proverbs was: If a gift is not shared, it seems to disappear. I say that if a gift is not also *claimed and accepted*, it disappears *for us*, but may become or remain a gift shared for and by others, at our expense. This is what has happened with some of the folktales of Rabbit and his cohorts: Bear, Fox, Lion, and others. They are recognized and claimed by many storytellers of European American (especially Southern) heritage, people whose elders also heard the stories told when they were children; they are known and loved in some regions of Europe, where the Disney version of the tar baby tale is still made available in video format. And they are unheard in some families of African American heritage, the heritage in which their traditions were born, and from which the stories grew. We must give our children all the gifts of their families' histories, for they deserve that foundation that is a tradition from the ancient *orature* of Africa.

Thus, I use the term Affrilachian for myself and my family, and, when I can, I share historical connections. And that is why I title this work, *Beyond the Briar Patch*. I am a child of a people who were bred and born there, a receptacle of ancestral tales, and a proud warrior-rabbit myself.

Just like Rabbit, I have grown beyond the briar patch. But I have never forgotten its berry-sweet treasures. Nor its thorns. I am not afraid to return to it for the sake of my children's knowledge of self, for my own stability in this quickly-changing world, and for my storytelling audiences.

STORY NOTES

*For those few who have never heard, seen, or read the story of Rabbit's adventure, when Rabbit is captured by the villains, Bear and Wolf, he tells them they can do anything they want to him, as long as they don't throw him into the place he appears to fear the most, the briar patch. He sorrowfully pleads and begs for death in any manner, except being thrown in the briar patch. Of course, it's a trick; Rabbit knows his way around the briar patch as well as he knows his way around his enemies.

1. *Star Trek: Insurrection*. Paramount Pictures, 1998.

2. "Carter Plantations" is my mother's way of referring to the plantation property at Carter's Grove, Virginia. According to her, we are descendants of the "nonwhite" (as they were sometimes called) children of the Carter family.

3. "Native American Mythology". www.godchecker.com/pantheon/native_american-mythology.php

4. R. Bruce Bickley, *Joel Chandler Harris*. (Boston: Twayne Publishers, 1978).

The Briar Patch and Beyond

Rabbit wasn't the only character to travel beyond the briar patch. You'll meet or be reintroduced to some others in this book. One of my favorites will be a fellow named Jack, whose ambition—or lack of it—lands him in and out of thorny troubles, too.

On a storytelling trip along winding roads, up and down richly green valleys, and alongside weathered stone hills in Kentucky, the conversations with fellow tellers in the car wandered backward to childhood memories. As I rode along, listening to others and sharing anecdotes and laughter, visions of the story-folks who populated that region and the settings of Affrilachian folktales played along the roadways. My thoughts followed four-legged critters in fables and pourquoi tales, two-legged protagonists in stories both tall and true, and both animals and people in folktales that traveled through centuries of spoken knowledge and wisdom. Like our highway, that circled bluffs and weaves along rivers, I knew that the characters of the briar patch found their way through the thorns and into places of hope beyond. I had already shared some of those stories in *Affrilachian Tales*, the first collection of narratives that friend and publisher Ted Parkhurst encouraged me to submit for publication.

I offer more of them within these pages, memories of childhood summers shared in storytelling with my father, Edward M. Cooper, and my maternal grandfather, "Pop-Pop" Byard

Wilmer Arkward, and bedtime-story readings with my mother, Jean E. Arkward Cooper Matthews. Those dear elders and many others gave me a treasure trove of folktales. Before I knew what folktales were, or that the ones I heard were rooted in the folk traditions of cultures from Africa, Europe, and the Americas, I was blessed with a very special library, a collection of literature preserved and presented in the oral tradition.

Years later, as I shared some of those stories with my own children, I felt a strong desire to know more about that special library. My attempts to retrieve, research, and revive tales that my own generation within my family may have begun to forget drew me into historical connections to the stories that my great-grandparents never told to children. The stories I found were tributes to cleverness, strength of mind and spirit, and occasionally homilies on the merits of a healthy curiosity. They included legends and humorous tales that reinforced the wisdom of a few stories my father had shared with me.

Some of the most enlightening stories carry cautionary messages of realities that young people have always faced at the hands of bad people.

I hope to honor my great-grandparents' tales of the briar patch eras of their parents' lives and their own childhoods. With respect for my father's storytelling, I have included Dad's versions of the legends of the wise and clever captive, sometimes known as John or Old John, sometimes called John the Conqueror. They were given to me in a second-hand manner, Daddy having told me he heard them as a child, or he "got them" from my great-grandfather. These were some of the stories that my grandmothers seemed to think we should forget or cast aside, "slave tales," that they considered demeaning and "low." The only shame I would ever associate with these stories would be their loss.

I know there is much more that can be shared from my very personal collection of Affrilachian folktales and lore. But some once-treasured stories have become dulled by time and fickle memory, including many of the spookers and haint tales. Perhaps another day the channel of memory may be clearer, allowing other stories through. It is a hazard of the oral tradition that some cultural jewels lie hidden or out of focus, awaiting some unknown hint to nudge them loose from that veiled shelf on which they rest. But I have shared a trio of spooky tales here. On this day, I don't remember all of the spookers. Indeed, in what remains of my lifetime, I may not gather all of them. Still, I will do what I can to keep my family's stories and story traditions alive.

I hope that other story-catchers and story-keepers continue to lift up their histories, write down their stories, and preserve the voices of diverse African-American Appalachian peoples. In remembrance of our ancestors, and for the sake of all the world's children, it is right that we should do so.

As I wrote in my first book, *Affrilachian Tales: Folktales from the African American Appalachian Tradition*, the term "Affrilachian" was created by poet, author, and educator Frank X. Walker, in response to a very clear denial of the populations and cultural traditions of African heritage within the Appalachian region. Had he not created that wonderful word, I wouldn't have the personal power found in knowing a "name" for "us;" knowing who "we" are commands recognition from others. I also would not have that title for my first story collection.

Stories need to be collected and honored and told again, again, and again. Thus, I share a second book of beloved Affrilachian folktales with you. You may find some childish and tickly, some tinged with shadows and touched by thorns. So be it. In some way, may your reading of them help you get through your own briar patch.

CRITTERS

You've met them before.

Rabbit.

Turtle.

Wolf.

Their very names call forth well-known character types. If you haven't met them, you probably know some critters that are like them, animals in fables and fictions that eventually became a part of Appalachia's diverse folk history. Some folks might be surprised that many of these stories were dressed in the *kente cloth* (*nwentoma*) patterns of the Ashanti, or *Malian bogolanfini* or "mud cloth" long before they wore the toga of Greece, or the stereotypical country overalls seen in illustrations for the adaptations of Joel Chandler Harris and the films of Disney Studios. Good stories sometimes change their clothes, but the body, the form and framework beneath them, remains pretty much the same.

Studying the Affrilachian tradition confirms the importance of appreciating the form of the character, just as it is appropriate to recognize and honor the heart of the tale. Both character and tale remind us of an ancestral soul in the telling. We honor early tellers by carrying on the art form—storytelling—that reminds each successive generation of the immutable laws of human nature.

The Happy Place
A Somewhat Different "Briar-Patch" Tale

Rabbit was on his way back home from one adventure or another. He was thinkin' about his wife and children, and all the joy in his family. Rabbit felt good, even better than good. His heart was happy beyond happy. The day sang to him, and the rising sun shone down so warm and lovin' that it put a big smile on his face.

Rabbit hopped and sang back to the day, "I'm goin' back to my happy place, goin' back to my happy place. Like fish in the water, like birds in the air, I'm happy in my happy place."

Rabbit had his nose in the air, as he hopped proudly and sang loudly. Mouth open, eyes closed, he couldn't see where he was goin'. And he hopped right into somebody big, and furry, and kind of growly.

It was Bear.

"Rabbit, where's this happy place?" growled Bear. "I need one right about now, 'cause I ain't happy this mornin'."

Bear didn't explain his unhappiness. He just glared at Rabbit.

"Well, I really don't know where your happy place is, Bear," Rabbit politely said. "I'm goin' to my happy place. Might not be the same place as yours."

"Then take me to yours, Rabbit. I'll just take your happy

place," said Bear. And he grinned a grin that showed his teeth, in a way that was anything but happy.

Rabbit thought about his good wife and his sweet children. "Bear," he said, "I can't take you to my happy place. You have to find your own!"

Bear stood even taller. He raised his paws and out sprang his claws. He opened his mouth and out came his bad breath. Bear growled, "Rrrrrrr … Take me to your happy place right now! Or I will change your name from 'Rabbit' to 'Breakfast!'"

Well, Rabbit didn't want to change his name. And he definitely didn't want to be called "Breakfast." But he couldn't take that mean and hungry beast to the place where his family safely waited for him. And, of course, bein' the kind of critter he was, Rabbit started thinkin' up a plan.

ᚦᚪ ᚪᚴ

It was only a second or three before Rabbit started walkin' alongside Bear, and singin' his song, " … I'm happy in my happy place."

Well, you know how some folks are when they're not happy? They have to make everybody else unhappy, too. Bear was one of those kind 'a folks. He started teasin' Rabbit and talkin' about him like he wasn't worth ever bein' born.

Bear snickered at Rabbit, looked him up and down, and said, "Yeah, I guess you need a happy place most days, Rabbit, 'cause nobody likes you or your kind. That's why you needed to find a happy place."

Rabbit just kept on walkin' along, singin' and smilin'.

Bear kept lookin' at Rabbit, and said, "I don't know why you got a smile on your face, Rabbit. You are one of the ugliest critters in the *holler*. Look at you, look at those big feet and those long ears and that funny li'l bunny-bun you got for a tail. Bet you needed a place to hide yourself, didn't you? That's why you needed a happy place."

Rabbit just kept on walkin' along, smilin' and singin'.

Bear laughed as he walked beside Rabbit, "Yeah, you are one pitiful ... ow. I mean, you got feet so big ... ouch ... I bet you trip over yourself ... ow ... everyday ... OUCH!"

Bear was so busy pickin' on that poor rabbit that he hadn't watched where he was bein' led. He was definitely bein' led somewhere. Somewhere poky!

By now he was deep in the briar patch, surrounded by thorny branches. Bear couldn't get himself out. He tried to pull his ears away from the thorns, but the fur caught and he hurt even more. Bear tried to yank his tail out of the thorns, but the fur tore and his eyes started to water. Bear cried out, "Rabbit, where ... where ... did you just lead me?"

Rabbit said, "Well, that depends on how you feel, Bear. Right now, how do you feel?"

Bear said, "Stuck."

Rabbit said, "Well, Bear, you want to know how I feel? I feel good, even better than good. My heart is happy beyond happy. The day is singin' to me, and the warm sun is settin' a smile on my face. "Ha! I guess, right at the moment, this is my happy place," Rabbit laughed.

Rabbit left Bear stuck in the briar patch, the place where Rabbit had been born. And he went on to his wife, his children, his family, his home, the joy that was really his happy place.

STORY NOTES

I've tried to give this story the voice of my favorite storyteller, Edward M. Cooper, known as "Jake," who was also my father. Although he could speak American business English as well as any businessman, his storytelling was often enriched by the oratorical language he shared with us, a cozy and easy transition into a kind of slang and twang that revealed Daddy's Tennessee roots. That manner of telling wasn't evident in all of his stories. I suspect that, when he told certain tales, he also shared the voice of the teller who gave the gift of that particular narrative to him.

I sometimes realize that same thing happening in my work, as well. In writing rather than telling this story, I felt a strong need to preserve its orature on the printed page. It seems only right to record a story heard orally with some of the teller's inflection and pacing intact.

This tale is a variant of the "laughing place" story collected by Joel Chandler Harris and titled "Brother Rabbit's Laughing-Place."[1] In that version, Rabbit tricks Brother Fox into seeking the laughing place in a thicket of dry bamboo briars, blackberry thorns, and honeysuckle. There was no mention of home and family.

But family was very important to my father, who worked two jobs to provide for us and help the extended family. Sundays were my dad's only full day off each week, but he spent the mornings in church, mid-day dinnertime with relatives, and afternoons mowing family lawns or weeding and planting family gardens—or repairing some aunt's television set. On a Sunday evening, it wasn't uncommon to find him re-wiring one of the clan's old homes, or even doing repairs at homes of friends, acquaintances, and community elders. All that weekend work never filled his wallet, but I think the act of helping others filled his heart to overflowing.

I believe that, no matter where he was or what he did, Dad was always in his happy place.

1. Joel Chandler Harris, *Told by Uncle Remus: New Stories of the Old Plantation*. (New York: McClure, Phillips & Company, 1905).

Turtle and Rabbit

Rabbit boasted all the time: "I am fast and fabulous, the finest critter in these woods! I've never lost a race down this here footpath, and I never will!"

Critters got tired of hearing Rabbit toot his own horn. They wished he'd shut his bragging lips, but he never did. Bragged all morning, into the afternoon, right on up to sun-goes-down. The poor critters couldn't get any rest, and they couldn't figure out how to get Rabbit to stop making so much noise about himself.

Then Turtle came up with a plan to stop Rabbit's bragging. That evening, he toddled to the footpath where Rabbit was still stomping his feet and bragging. Turtle spoke in his slow and steady way, "Rabbit, you and I … will race … down the footpath … tomorrow. If you win … I'll give up … my favorite … place to rest … in the sun … on the flat rocks … next to … the river. If I win … you have to … give up your … braggin' ways."

Rabbit thought this was the funniest thing he had ever heard. He laughed so hard his tail nearly popped off his backside. But Rabbit agreed to race against Turtle, first thing in the morning.

Early the next morning, Turtle and Rabbit and all the other critters got themselves into position for the race. Turtle and Rabbit stood at a line in the dust of the footpath at the edge of the forest. Big Boss Lion, who was going to be the judge, waited at the finish line, the rocks next to the river. Some critters waited with him. The other critters stood around Turtle and Rabbit, and waited to call out for the race to begin.

When the sun pushed itself up over the trees, all kinds of critters growled and howled and tweeted and hissed to get things started, "One for the money, two for the show, three to get ready, and four to ... go, go, **GO!**"*

Rabbit zipped away from the starting line, *ZIP!*, and down the footpath. He had already disappeared into the woods, when Turtle managed to lift one foot at the starting line.

"Here ... I ... go," said Turtle. "Whew ... I am ... really ... moving!"

Rabbit was getting close to a big rock. There was no sign of Turtle behind him. Rabbit chuckled, and sang, "Turtle, Turtle, slow, slow, Turtle! Turtle, Turtle, where are you?"

Beside the rock, somebody else sang, "Here ... I ... am! Run ... Rabbit! Run ... run ... run!"

It was Turtle!

Rabbit hollered, "Turtle? How did you get to this rock before I did?"

Turtle just grinned, didn't say anything more. Up jumped Rabbit. He took off and ran even faster than he'd been running. And Rabbit passed Turtle, *WHOOSH!*

Down that footpath sped Rabbit. He was getting close to a blackberry bush, and he was getting kind of weary and awfully hungry. Rabbit stopped to catch his breath. Then he stretched his legs a bit, and nibbled on some berries.

Rabbit laughed, "Ha! I know Turtle is far behind me now!"

And Rabbit sang, "Turtle, Turtle, slow, slow Turtle! Turtle, Turtle, where are you?"

Underneath the blackberry bush, somebody else sang a different song, "Here ... I ... am! Run ... Rabbit! Run ... run ... run!"

Oh, no, thought Rabbit, Turtle had somehow passed him again!

Rabbit hollered, "Turtle!?! You don't even sound tired! How did you get ahead of me?" Rabbit jumped a couple times, to get his motor revved up. Then he passed Turtle, *ZOOM!*

Rabbit ran faster that he had ever run in his life, but he was running out of *gumption*. Soon he was too tired to laugh and too hoarse to sing. Rabbit could hardly breathe, "Huh … uh … huh … uh … huh." He thought he was winning the race, so he started walking toward the rocks at the edge of the river, "Huh … uh … huh … uh … huh." His knees ached, his feet hurt. Even his ears were in pain.

Rabbit stumbled closer to the finish line. He could see the river. He could see the flat rocks where Turtle liked to rest. He could see the judge, Big Boss Lion, resting on those rocks. He could also see somebody else, somebody small, sitting beside Big Boss Lion.

And you know who it was? That's right, it was Turtle!

Animals giggled as Big Boss Lion roared, "Rabbit, you movin' a little slow this mornin'. You know what that means? It means … Turtle WINS!"

Rabbit's ears flopped down. His head hung low. He pouted a bit, then he dragged himself on home. He didn't do any hopping all the rest of that day. And Rabbit never boasted again. In fact, Rabbit hasn't said much of anything since that race.

Turtle thanked Big Boss Lion and all the other critters for their kind support. He held his head high as he walked back up the footpath. And at the blackberry bush, he met Sis Turtle.

They walked to the big rock. Beside the rock, they met Mama Turtle.

The Turtle family made their way to the starting line. There stood Granddaddy Turtle. He'd managed to get that one foot up to start the race. Then he'd fallen asleep.

See, everybody in the Turtle family looked the same. They all sounded the same, too. But Rabbit didn't know that.

Turtle, with his family's help, won the race. That was the end of Rabbit's bragging.

That's the end of this story, too.

STORY NOTES

*This phrase probably has its roots in the win, place, and show bets of horse racing. It was seen in print in 1872, on page 14 of a book called *Striking for the Right* (Lothrop), by Julia Arabella Eastman.

Of course, most folks are acquainted with the fable of "Tortoise and Hare." It is attributed to Aesop of Greece, but that's not the whole story of the story.

There is truth in every story. But the reality of Aesopic fables is that their teller may not have existed. He is said to have lived around 620–560 BC, and is referenced by Plato and Heroditus. Supposedly, Socrates, jailed and awaiting his trial and eventual death for corrupting youth by sharing his views and by expressing impiety ("failing to acknowledge the gods that the city acknowledges" and "introducing new deities"[1]), passed the time creating verses from the fables of Aesop.

Aesop was described in *The Aesop Romance*, an anonymous work of fiction from the 1st or 2nd Century A.D., as an ugly and silent Phrygian slave on the island of Samos who was given the powers of speech and storytelling after he showed kindness to a priestess of Isis. His life was a fable of success. In the Middle Ages, he was described as a black Ethiopian,[2] whose name, Aethiop, supposedly proved his connection to the continent and stories of Africa; the proofs for Aesop's ethnicity, and his existence, are still being argued. But the connections to folktales in both Asia and Africa are evident simply by reading stories collected in the Jataka tales, the Panchatantra, and the many collections of folktales from East, West, South, and Central Africa.

Now, what does all of that have to do with the Affrilachian twist to the story of the tortoise and the hare? In the versions of the tale of the race between the swift and the steady that I have read in anthologies or heard told by a handful of tellers born in diverse African cultures, the moral of the story is not "slow and steady wins the race."

The moral is "Unity is strength."

From the tales of the Khoikhoi of southern Africa comes a variant in which Hare crosses the sands of the Kalahari Desert and loses the race to the relatives of Tortoise who are stationed long the designated path. From the Yoruba language of Nigeria, Benin, and Togo we have the tale of Elephant, Tortoise, and Hare, in Jack Berry's collection, *West African Folk Tales*[3], he presents the same story, with a few other animals in the race. And Joel Chandler Harris published this version of the animal's race as "Mr. Rabbit Finds His Match at Last,"[4] in a competition that directly reflects the Bantu storytelling influence. Julius Lester renames this version "Brer Rabbit Gets Beaten,"[5] and includes references to the speed of a 747 jet and spectators drinking Dr. Pepper. The contemporary enhancements in no way disguise the roots of the retelling.

Some folks—especially children in classes from kindergarten through second grade—would say Tortoise and his family cheated. Within the confines of athletic competition, their simple interpretation would be morally correct. Traditionally, however, the story carries a much wider focus: the "race" of life. In that broadest context, survival is the highest value. The family bond, essential to survival in nearly every environment, is the fundamental value. *What would you do to save your family or community from a bully?* I repeat: Unity is strength.

1. I. F. Stone, *The Trial of Socrates*. (New York: Little, Brown, 1988).

2. Frank M. Snowden, Jr., *Blacks in Antiquity: Ethiopians in the Greco-Roman Experience*. (Cambridge: Harvard University Press, 1970).

3. Jack Berry, *West African Folk Tales*. (Northwestern University Press, 1991).

4. Joel Chandler Harris, *Uncle Remus: His Songs and Sayings*. (New York: D. Appleton & Company, 1880).

5. Lester, Julius, 1987. *The Tales of Uncle Remus: The Adventures of Brer Rabbit*. (New York: Dial Books, 1987).

Grasshopper and the Ants

The ants were marching along in a line, working together to gather things they needed for their home, getting that ant hill filled with what they needed to survive the winter. And as they marched along, the ants sang their working song:

Work, work, work, work, work, work, work, work ...

They passed a grasshopper on that fine spring day. He watched them all marching, and all working, all marching, and all working. The grasshopper shouted at them, "Hey! What you doin'?"

The ants said, "Work!"

Well, this grasshopper didn't know what work was. He'd never done it. You might know some folks like that grasshopper.

He said, "Work? *What is that?* And why are you doin' it?"

The ants said, "Because, we're gettin' ready for winter!"

The grasshopper didn't know what winter was, either. He laughed and sang,

Work, winter, winter, work, well ...
you do that work, do that work, do that work, aw, do that work,

but play and sing, play and sing,
I'll just play and sing, yeah!

And that's what the grasshopper did all through the spring. But, then, something happened.

The sun shone brighter and the days were warmer. Things grew, tall and green, in gardens. It was summer, and out of their anthill popped the ants.

They marched along together, gathering things for winter, and as they marched along, they sang their working song,

Work, work, work, work, work, work, work, work ...

They passed that same grasshopper, standing in a field of low corn. The grasshopper asked again, "Hey! What you doin'?"

The ants said, "Work!"

The grasshopper said, "Again? Why?"

The ants said, "Because we're gettin' ready for *winter!*"

Well, that grasshopper still didn't know a thing about work or winter. He shook his head, laughed and said,

Work, winter, winter, work, well ...
you do that work, do that work, do that work, aw, do that work,
but play and sing, play and sing,
I'll just play and sing, yeah!

The grasshopper didn't do one bit of planning or work.

Then, something happened. Winds *blew* and clouds *grew,* and leaves fell from the trees. It was autumn, and out of their anthill popped the ants.

They marched along together, gathering things for winter, and as they marched along, they sang their working song,

Work, work, work, work, work, work, work, work ...

They passed that very same grasshopper; he was standing in a pile of leaves. He saw the ants. He asked again, "Hey! What you doin' now?"

And, again, the ants said, "Work!"

"Still?" said the grasshopper. "Why?"

The ants said, "Because, we're gettin' ready for WINTER!"

Some folks just don't educate themselves. That grasshopper still didn't know about winter or work. But he did know about laughing and singing. That's what he did. He laughed at the ants, and he sang,

Work, winter, winter, work, well …
you do that work, do that work, do that work, aw, do that work,
but play and sing, play and sing,
I'll just play and sing, yeah!

He didn't lift a finger to do one bit of work himself. Then, something happened.

The wind blew harder, the clouds grew bigger. The days got colder. And as the grasshopper stood alone in a forest where the trees were bald and bare, something cold, wet, and white fell from the sky and landed on his head.

It was snow. And it was winter!

"Brrrr, "said the grasshopper, "What was that?"

Something cold, wet, and white landed on his head again. But you know that grasshopper didn't know about winter or snow.

"Brrrr," he said, "What was *that*?"

More snow fell, then more snow fell, and after a while, that grasshopper was covered from head to toe with snow. He looked like a little grasshopper snowman, with nothing but his eyes and his mouth showing. He couldn't ask questions, or laugh, or sing. All he could do was stand there covered in snow and say, "Brrrr …"

That's the way the grasshopper stayed all through the

winter. Then, something happened.

The winds changed and blew the clouds away. The sun shone a little brighter that day. Buds popped out on bushes and trees. Grass popped out of the ground, and, out of their anthill popped the ants.

They started marching along together, working together to gather things for their home, getting that anthill filled with what they needed for the winter. And, as they marched along, they sang that same song,

Work, work, work, work, work, work, work, work ...

By that time, the grasshopper had thawed out. And when he saw the ants all working together, he didn't ask questions, or laugh, or song. My Pop-Pops said that grasshopper got right at the end of the line, started marching with those ants, started singing that song,

Work, work, work, work, work, work, work, work ...

He had finally figured something out. Sometimes there's work that must be done.

But when the work is done, there's usually some time to play and sing, play and sing. Work, *then* play and sing, yeah!

STORY NOTES

Okay, this is a little-kids version of the well-known fable. My grandfather told it, with repetition, rhythm and rhyme, but I added the "yeah!" at the end of the grasshopper's ditty. And Pop-Pops laughed.

He knew that I hated stories in which someone or something died. I couldn't stand the Disney movie, "Bambi," and I've only seen it once in my entire life, because, as I told my own mother, "They killed Bambi's mother!" And I was angry with the tornado that dropped a house on the Wicked Witch in *The Wizard of OZ*. Didn't matter that she was wicked. That house simply should not have fallen on the Wicked Witch of the East's poor mean ole' body! And then, adding insult to injury, Dorothy stole her shoes!!!

So the grasshopper never froze to death in Pop-Pops version of "The Grasshopper and the Ants." And the Big Bad Wolf always survived the Woodsman in "Red Riding Hood." Actually, there was no Woodsman in my grandfather's version of the story. The wolf shoved Granny into the closet, put on her nightie, and tried to trick and gobble up Little Red. But Granny jumped out of the closet, and blew off Big Bad's tail with her hunting rifle, BOOM! End of his tail, end of the story.

But the Big Bad Wolf lived.

I got in trouble with my kindergarten and first grade teachers, letting them know they didn't know the correct way to tell stories. They hadn't listened to my daddy or Pop-pop, whose stories were always better.

My teachers also didn't seem to understand that you didn't stop the work of the day to tell a story. You might tell or sing while you worked, but you wouldn't stop the spelling work or the reading work to tell a story, anymore than you would stop the work in the garden or the kitchen or the yard. It simply was not done.

Nowadays, I wish more folks gave young ones stories, any day, every day, anytime they could.

Next, one more fable, for the ears of the bigger folks …

Fox and Crow

Some folks used to say that Vanity's name was Woman. But the critters knew that couldn't be right. If anyone were to speak truth in those once-upon-a-times, he or she would have said what the critters knew: Vanity, thy name is Miz Crow.

Seems like Miz Crow had been born bragging, calling out to anyone who could hear, "Caw-lin' awl y'all to look at me! Caw-lin' awl y'all!" She would strut, and pose, and call again, "Caw-lin' awl y'all!"

Most critters went in the other direction. Who would want to approach all the audacious noise coming out of that windbag of a bird? Nobody. Until the day Fox was hungry, and Miz Crow flew by holding a beakful of corn *fritter* she'd stolen off some poor cook's breakfast table.

The fritter was warm, and smelled of butter and bacon grease. Fox knew what it was without really seeing it. He drooled as he followed its aroma to the trunk of a tulip tree. Up in the high branches of that tree sat Miz Crow, with the fritter still in her beak.

Oh, Fox wanted that fritter!

Now, how was he going to get that tasty treat? Hunger brought an idea to Fox's brain quicker than you can say "braggadocio." Fox put on his sugar-syrup smile, and shouted up into the big leaves of that tulip tree, "Why, what did I just see? Was it an angel that flew past me? Oh, no, there she is, up there on that branch, gracing us all with her beauty! Why, it's that sweet-voiced wonder, Miz Crow!"

Miz Crow sat a bit taller, pumped her chest out, and grinned. But she held onto that fritter.

Fox shouted again. "Miz Crow, you sing songs that put the sparrows to shame! Why, you sing melodies Miz Mockingbird wouldn't dare to try! Miz Crow, you are truly a wonder. You do shake a pretty wing, but you sing even better!"

Miz Crow sat up even straighter, and puffed her chest so far out that she had to lift her head to breathe. But she held onto that fritter.

Fox moaned, "Oh, Miz Crow. I came to this tree, anticipating hearing a glorious tune. And, look at you, you got your beak in the air, and you won't even whisper a note! I am beyond disappointed, I am devastated!"

Fox pretended to cry, "Oh, I am, *sniff, sniff*—simply, *sniff, sniff*—and completely, *sniff, sniff*—devastated!"

Well, Miz Crow couldn't keep disappointing her audience. She looked down at Fox, opened her beak, and called, "Caw-lin' awl y'all to look at me! Caw-lin' awl y'all!"

The corn fritter fell out of her mouth, and flopped right into Fox's. Gulp!

"Thank you, Miz Crow!" Fox shouted up to that surprised and saddened bird. And with that, Fox trotted off to find another meal.

ú ɬ

CORN FRITTERS

1 large can (15-16 ounces) corn, well-drained

3 eggs

½ - ¾ cup milk or buttermilk

½ teaspoon salt

⅛ cup sugar

1 – 1¼ cup flour

1 – 1¼ cup self-rising corn meal baking mix (I like Aunt Jemima's white corn meal mix, but I guess any

Self-rising corn meal mix is okay)

Bacon grease for frying

Beat the drained corn, eggs and ½ cup milk in a medium-sized bowl. Blend the salt, sugar, flour, and corn meal baking mix, then slowly add the combined dry ingredients to the corn/egg mixture. Mix well with a large spoon until batter is fairly smooth (except for the corn, of course); add about ¼ cup milk if needed to make batter smoother. Heat about 2 or 3 tablespoons of bacon grease in a large skillet (cast iron, if you have one) over medium high heat. When the grease is hot, drop in the fritters by spoonfuls (a large tablespoon works well). Fry until golden brown. After they have browned on one side, turn and brown the other side. Remove from pan and drain on paper towels. Transfer them to a warm plate.

Serve at once with butter and syrup.*

STORY NOTES

*This was one of those recipes that had to be translated from "handfuls", "tads", "bits", and "smidgens" to cans, cups, and spoonfuls. You'll have to adapt it to your own tastes, just like any other down-home cook would do. You won't regret the perfection of your own version of the final product!

On a recent storytelling road trip in Kentucky, in a car filled with naturally gifted storytellers, I heard another version of one of the "teaching tales" that I remember from my childhood. I laughed so hard I thought I'd get car-sick as fellow traveler Sasikumar Balasundaram, or "Sasi" for short, shared his adventures trying to order food at a Subway restaurant when he first arrived in South Carolina. He told us about the long walks to and from school when he was a boy in Sri Lanka, and of the South Carolina culture shock of mistaking the North American marsupial and star of many Affrilachian and Appalachian folktales, Possum, for a rat. A BIG rat!

Dr. Balasundaram, a postdoctoral scholar at the University of Kentucky Appalachian Center, claimed he wasn't a storyteller, then proceeded to tell me a story he said was known by every grandmother in Sri Lanka. Although he was sitting behind me in the car, I could sense the story unfolding from his mind and heart and flowing through his voice. It was easy to imagine myself as a child sitting at my own great-grandmother's feet, as Sasi spoke of the character who, in his version, held a doughnut in her mouth, and was outwitted by a fox who requested her "beautiful" song and retrieved her dropped morsel when the flattered crow opened her beak to sing. Yes, Sasi's folktale sparked that memory, and I had to add my family's version of "Fox and Crow" to this manuscript. Doing so, I am aware that Aesop's version spoke of cheese, just as in my family's version the morsel had morphed into corn fritter, and I smile knowing that corn fritters are closer to doughnuts than cheese. While the progression of folklore around the world is certainly not linear, perhaps it arches toward similarity.

When I was a child, I didn't pick up on this fable's most-commonly accepted moral: never trust a flatterer. It seemed to me there were two other lessons in the tale. The first was: don't brag and boast. The second was: don't talk with your mouth full. I had heard that particular admonition many, many times.

I have long been aware that the story has its better-known moral. Yet, I think my forebears told the story to me more for fun than to teach me about flattery, ego, or even talking with my mouth full. My grandfather told the story, and Pop-Pops was definitely not the person to teach lessons about vanity.

Pop-Pops never left the house looking anything but "good." He dyed his hair, keeping it a glistening black, shinier than a crow's wing. When I was five, Pop-Pops' hair was black. When I was fifteen, my Daddy's hair was gray, but Pop-pop's was still black.

But the silver tresses began to powerfully outnumber the black ones, making the expense and duration of his hair treatments exponentially increase. Pop-Pops creatively took the situation into his own hands; even though Grandma Josephine was a hairdresser, Pop-Pops personally and privately enhanced his image. Apparently, he was going for what he thought was a dignified, maturely handsome look. He dyed the middle part of his hair and the part above each ear with a rich, jet black coloring, leaving a broad white streak on either side of his head.

He was proud of his newly enhanced appearance. Grandma Josephine was not. And I was simply dumbfounded.

Did you ever see Grandpa Munster in that old television show, or the regal vampires in old B-movies? Pop-Pops reminded me of them; I wanted to buy him a cape. But no seriously self-respecting bloodsucker would've let his hair look like my grandfather's. In fact, the look was much less like "Nosferatu" and much more like "Pepe Le Pew," the cartoon skunk.

Still, you could not convince him that he didn't look good. On Sunday, in his perfectly polished black patent-leather loafers, his expensively tailored suit and silk tie, with his black onyx tie-tack and cufflinks shining in their gold settings, Pop-Pops walked into church with his head held high, shaking and showing off that hair like a dozen gold chains. He sat proudly. He stood tall. He belted out every hymn loudly and proudly.

He sang like Miz Crow. And you didn't hear me say that.

Vanity, thy name was Pop-Pops. But there was nothing wrong with his storytelling!

Mrs. Turtle's Cooking Pot

Once upon a time, 'bout time and a half ago, turtles didn't look the way they do now. They didn't have those shells on their backs, and they walked around like people. They talked like people, lived in houses like people, too. And they slept in beds and ate their meals with forks and spoons, just like people, got hungry for breakfast just like people.

Turtle woke up one morning with a *simenjous* hunger. He stretched. He breathed deep, and he knew he was gonna have a good breakfast. His nose told him that Mrs. Turtle was making his favorite soup!

"Oooh," said Turtle, "I'm gonna have some soup for breakfast, a mess of soup for supper, a little more soup for dinner, maybe have soup for dessert, maybe even have soup for midnight snack, too! Oh, I love soup!"

But when Turtle walked into the kitchen, he got a little worried. The smell of good soup wasn't coming from his kitchen, for there wasn't a smidgen of soup or anything else cooking there. There was no cooking going on in that kitchen, and Mrs. Turtle was nowhere in sight. Still, there was that wonderful aroma ...

Turtle followed that smell right out the kitchen door and into the backyard. There was Mrs. Turtle, standing over a big ol' cooking pot that hung on a tripod over a big ol' fire. Mrs. Turtle stirred the contents of that pot with her biggest wooden stirring spoon. The sight made Turtle happy.

But, what Mrs. Turtle was singing gave him pause. Her song did more than that, it made Turtle downright upset. Mrs. Turtle was singing,

My mother is coming, my mother is coming, my mother is coming to visit to day.

"Oh, no," Turtle muttered to himself, "My mother-in-law is comin' to visit. That woman can eat some soup. Why, when she finishes slurpin' up her fill at suppertime, there may not be enough soup left to fill a teaspoon for dinner. And there definitely won't be anything left for dessert.

"If I'm gonna get some soup, I better get it right now," thought Turtle. But he knew that Mrs. Turtle wasn't gonna let him taste that soup until her mother got there. Now, maybe, if he found a way to trick her into letting him have a bowl or two.

Hmmm ....

Turtle walked over to his good wife. He put on his most loving smile, and said in his sweetest voice, "Good mornin,' darlin' dear."

Mrs. Turtle stopped stirring that soup long enough to smile at her husband. "Why, good morning, Mr. Turtle!" she said, as a wide smile crossed her face.

"My dear, sweet Missus, what you cookin' in that pot?" Turtle asked.

Mrs. Turtle was surprised. "Why, can't you tell by the smell, Mr. Turtle? I'm making your favorite soup!"

Turtle got really close to that cooking pot, and sniffed a big sniff. Oh, it smelled sooo good, but Turtle lied, "No, I can't smell nothin', Mrs. Turtle. You better let me taste it to see if it tastes like my favorite soup."

Mrs. Turtle said, "Okay, fine." She picked up a little bowl

from the table where she was keeping her utensils. She handed the bowl to Turtle. Then she gave him a teaspoon. Then, with her wooden stirring spoon, Mrs. Turtle scooped out some of that soup and plopped it into the bowl.

Well, Turtle tasted a little bit with that teaspoon. Oh, oh, oh, it was good! He filled the teaspoon again. Oh, me, oh, my, the soup was heavenly! Turtle tipped the bowl to his lips and drank the rest of the soup, "SSSlurp!" Oh, that soup was a gastronomic miracle!

But Turtle said, "I'm not sure if this is good enough, Mrs. Turtle. I heard you say your mother is coming. This soup might not be good enough for her.

"Better let me have another taste, to see if it's good enough for your mother."

Mrs. Turtle said, "Okay, fine." She scooped out some more of that soup and plopped it into Turtle's bowl.

Turtle took a little with the teaspoon, then a lot, then he just tipped that bowl and slurped, "SSSlurp!" Oh, his toes curled at the taste of it!

But Turtle said, "No, there's something wrong with this soup, Mrs. Turtle. Seems like something is missing from the flavor. You better let me have a little bit more, so I can figure out what's missing."

This time, Mrs. Turtle thought a bit. Then she said, "No, Turtle, you've had enough to taste what's wrong. You just smack your lips a bit, see what you think is missing."

Turtle was disappointed, but he had another idea growing in his head. He smacked his lips, smack, smack, smack. Then Turtle said, "Hmm, I taste carrots and cabbage, peppers and peas, onions and okra, potatoes and parsnips, but I think I know what's missing now. Mrs. Turtle, dear, I think this soup needs more salt."

"Salt?" Mrs. Turtle put down her stirring spoon, and picked up a small salt shaker from the table. "I put a little salt in the soup," she said.

"A little salt ain't tasty enough, honey, and you want it to be tasty enough for your mother," said Turtle. "You better get the big salt shaker from the kitchen, shake some more salt in that soup."

Mrs. Turtle said, "Okay, fine." She set down that little salt shaker, and headed for the kitchen to get the big salt shaker that was in the cupboard. As she walked, Mrs. Turtle sang,

My mother is coming, my mother is coming, my mother is coming to visit today.

When Turtle couldn't hear her voice anymore, he knew Mrs. Turtle was too far inside the house to see what he was doing outside it. Turtle set down his bowl and teaspoon on the little table, grabbed the sides of the pot, and tipped it toward his face. Turtle stuck his head in that pot, and started drinking up the soup, gulp, gulp, gobble, gobble …

Then he heard a song coming closer to the kitchen door, and the yard beyond it. Mrs. Turtle was coming back!

Turtle straightened out the pot on its hook, wiped the soup from his mouth with his hands, hid his hands behind his back, and smiled his best I-have-just-been-standing-here-doing-nothing smile.

Mrs. Turtle walked past him, and got ready to shake a *passel* of salt into the cooking pot.

But the soup was perfect! And Turtle didn't want it ruined. He shouted, "Stop, Mrs. Turtle! I was wrong. The soup doesn't need salt. What it needs is pepper."

"Pepper?" Mrs. Turtle shook her head. "Now, Mr. Turtle, I already put a little pepper in the soup!"

"Not enough," said Turtle. "Mrs. Turtle, dear, you know your mother likes spicy food. You need to put more pepper in the soup. In fact, you should get the black pepper and the red pepper, and chop a few of those little hot peppers to put in it. Then it will be perfect for your mother!"

Mrs. Turtle said, "Okay, fine." She walked back toward the kitchen, and she sang as she walked,

My mother is coming, my mother is coming, my mother is coming to visit today.

When Turtle couldn't hear the song anymore, he knew where Mrs. Turtle was, far enough away from him to not hear what he was about to do.

Turtle tipped the pot toward his face again, stuck his head into that soup, and drank, gulp, gulp, gobble, gobble, gobble ...

Then he heard that song, and he knew Mrs. Turtle was coming. Turtle straightened the pot on its hook, wiped his mouth with his hands, hid his hands behind his back, and smiled his best I-am-as-innocent-as-a-newborn-baby smile.

Mrs. Turtle walked past him. He saw that she was carrying two pepper shakers and a bowl filled with chopped hot peppers. Oh, no, that heat would ruin the soup!

Turtle shouted, "Stop, Mrs. Turtle! I was wrong. The soup doesn't need any peppers in it. It's spicy enough. What it needs is ... uh, is ... uh ... what it needs is something that would surprise your mother, something she would never expect to find in a pot of soup ...

"I know," said Turtle. "Go and get a pair of socks and put them in the soup."

"A pair of socks?!" Mrs. Turtle was aghast. "Now, why in the name of Creation would I put a pair of socks in my soup?"

"Well, dear, your mother loves surprises. She couldn't get a bigger surprise than a pair of socks in her soup. Why, imagine how she'll laugh at that. Your mother loves to laugh almost as much as she loves soup!"

"Mrs. Turtle sighed, "Well ..."

"See if you can find a pair of those plaid socks. Go to the neighbors and see if anybody has a pair. Plaid socks would really surprise your mother! Oh, how she would laugh!!!" Turtle laughed a bit himself, more at the trick he was playing on his wife than at the thought of his mother-in-law laughing.

After a little thought, Mrs. Turtle said, "Okay ... fine."

Off she went to borrow a pair of plaid socks from some neighbor. Nervously, she sang,

My mother is coming, my mother is coming, my mother is coming to visit today.

Mrs. Turtle's voice disappeared around the side of the house. Turtle grabbed the sides of that cooking pot, tipped it to his face, stuck his head into the pot, and drank, gulp, gulp, gobble, gobble, gobble, gobble ...

He figured it would be a while before Mrs. Turtle came back. Plaid socks would be hard to find. Sooo ... Gulp, gulp, gobble, gobble, gobble, gobble, gobble ...

Turtle stopped to catch his breath. He listened. Nope, no song yet. Gulp, gulp, gobble, gobble, gobble, gobble, gobble, BURP!

Turtle stopped to excuse himself, a habit of good manners Mrs. Turtle had taught him. That's when he heard,

My mother is coming, my mother is coming ...

Oh, Mrs. Turtle was finally coming back! Turtle straightened that cooking pot on its hook. It seemed a bit light. He looked inside the pot. He saw the bottom of the pot. Turtle had eaten everything in that pot!

"Oh, I can't smile big enough or sweet enough to get out of this trouble!" Turtle said to himself. He looked around for a place to hide. There wasn't one, not a tree, not a bush. Oh, why hadn't he planted a tree or a bush in the backyard?

Then Turtle got an idea. He took the cooking pot off its hook over the fire. He quickly crouched down and put the hot pot over his body, pulled in his arms and his legs, and stayed very still. He sweated a rainstorm, but he stayed very still.

Mrs. Turtle was coming around the side of the house. In each hand was an argyle sock she had borrowed from a neighbor. She was thinking about whether or not she should put those socks in the soup.

But the cooking pot wasn't hanging on its hook over the fire. It was upside down on the ground. And there wasn't a puddle or a trickle or a drop of soup seeping from that big pot, no sign that there had been any soup cooking for her mother.

There wasn't any sign of Turtle in the backyard, either.

Mrs. Turtle dropped those socks. She walked over to her little table and picked up her wooden stirring spoon. Mrs. Turtle yelled at the cooking pot, "Turtle, are you hiding under my cooking pot?"

Without thinking, Turtle yelled, "No! Oh, uh-oh ..."

"And, Turtle, did you eat all that soup?"

Turtle stuck his head out from under the soup. There was no point in trying to lie, and no point in smiling, either. No smile would be big enough or innocent enough or sweet enough to get him out of this predicament. Turtle sighed, and quietly said, "Yeah."

Mrs. Turtle screamed, "Turtle, how could you be so greedy? That soup was for my mother's visit! There was enough soup for breakfast, and for supper, and for dinner, and maybe for dessert. Turtle, I ought to turn YOU into soup!"

And, with all her might and all her anger, Mrs. Turtle hit that big cooking pot with her wooden stirring spoon, Ka-WONGGGGGG! She hit it so hard, the spoon broke and the pot cracked.

Turtle shuddered underneath that cooking pot, "Uh-h-h-h-h ..."

"Now," Mrs. Turtle frowned and said very quietly and very slowly, "Come ... out ... from under ... that ... cooking pot."

Turtle said, "Okay, fine."

But he couldn't get out from under that pot. He could push out his arms and his legs, but the cracked pot was stuck to his back.

"Oh, Mrs. Turtle, I'm stuck," he whimpered. "I can't get out from under this pot!"

Mrs. Turtle felt so sorry for her husband, she dropped that broken spoon and apologized, "Oh, Turtle, I am sorry. I shouldn't have lost my temper. Let me get that thing off your back."

Well, Mrs. Turtle pulled and tugged and tugged and pulled, but the cooking pot stayed where it was. Mrs. Turtle couldn't release her husband from that pot, but she thought she might be able to help him feel better.

While Turtle cried and moaned, Mrs. Turtle went into the kitchen and got another cooking pot. She carried it outside and crouched down low, and pulled that cooking pot down on her back. She walked around, wearing that pot, and her best I-love-you smile.

"Look, Mr. Turtle, dear," she said. I'm wearing a cooking pot, too. She danced around and laughed. Pretty soon, Mr. Turtle was laughing, too.

When Mrs. Turtle's mother arrived, she asked, "Children, why are you walking around the backyard with cooking pots on your backs?"

Feeling foolish and more than a little embarrassed, Turtle lied, "Oh, this is the latest fashion for turtles. Soon everyone will be wearing cooking pots!"

When Mrs. Turtle's mother heard that, she walked right into the kitchen, pulled out a pot, and put it on her back.

Ever since then, turtles have walked around with cooking pots on their backs.

And if that's not true, it should be.

ᕕᕗ ᕘᕚ

STORY NOTES

This is a favorite *pourquoi* (how and why) tale. I hadn't told it in years. When I told it again for the first time, I added a song for the children to whom I was telling, a chorus for Turtle's greedy gobbling: Gulp gulp, gobble gobble, gulp gulp, gobble gobble, gulp gulp, gobble gobble, yum, yum, yum! Mrs. Turtle had a song. It seemed fitting to give Mr. Turtle a song, too. The words I sang are the words spoken when this tale was told to me.

That closing sentence, "And if that's not true, it should be," was Pop-pops way of letting me know he had stretched an already imaginative tale to its limit.

Pop-Pops also said Turtle ate vegetable soup. Sometimes he went over the ingredients: chicken or beef broth, potatoes, carrots, onions, celery, green beans, peas and corn. Except for the chicken or beef stock, it was all garden-grown. When Mama combined vegetables like that in a stock pot and they simmered for hours, the resulting soup was always delicious. If there was a soup bone in there, the goodness might simmer on a very low heat for what seemed like all day.

As for the socks in my version of the story: I turned them into stinky socks from the feet of some child who forgot to scrub his or her toes. That always gets a laugh. But that wasn't in Pop-Pops' version of the tale. And my grandfather never described those socks as "argyles." He just called them "plaid." He had a few pairs of plaid socks that he wore with his suits. He also had bright red socks, yellow socks, and black socks with his initials embroidered on them in silver or gold letters.

I told you the man was vain. Yep, right down to his socks.

I also told you he was a very good storyteller.

Pig's Nose

In the first days of Creation, when things hadn't quite settled into the way they would be, and Man and Woman were still just a twinkle in His eye, the Good Lord walked around tending to things Himself. He fed the littlest critters, checked on the behavior of the biggest ones, made sure the medium-sized critters had their say, and saw to it that everybody found a safe way to live.

It was hard work. That's why, by the sundown of the sixth day, the Good Lord needed to get a good night's rest.

But on that very evening, He realized that one of those newly-made critters was causing a heap of trouble, and enough of it to keep Him from going to sleep. That ornery critter was the one folks now call Pig.

See, in those first days, Pig didn't look the way he does now. He was a decent-sized fella, pink and chubby, but he had a straight tail, stuck out like an arrow pointing to where he had been. And he had a long, long nose like a baby elephant's trunk.

That nose was the problem.

The Good Lord was finishing up his work, feeding the littlest of the critters before sundown. He went to the river and flung out some fish food, seeds and bits of chopped-up vegetables. That fish food flew out of His great hand toward the water. But before one fish could smack his lips on those tidbits, Pig ran down to the edge of the river from wherever he had been, and used his long nose like a vacuum cleaner, sucked all the seeds and vegetable pieces into his fat face and right down his throat.

Well, the Good Lord snatched up that critter and carried him to the tree stump, the first tree cutting, made so that He would have a place to sit and take a break from His work. Good Lord didn't set Himself on the stump. He set that pig on it instead, and scolded him like any father might do.

"You already been fed, child, fed two or three times, in fact. You just bein' greedy. Now, you sit there on my stump, and you stay there outta my way 'til I get my work done, you hear?"

Pig pouted, but he said, "Yes, sir." And he sat on that stump, while the Good Lord commenced to feeding those fish. Then Pig smelled something else with that long nose he was wearing.

It smelled quite good, *sufficiently seransifyin'*. Pig jumped off that stump, and headed in the direction his nose was leading him.

There was the Good Lord, casting corn and seeds and bits of fruit and vegetables on the ground for the tiniest of the birds. And there was a big ol' nose, sucking up the morsels before one bird could peck a piece of it. Pig cleaned up that food in a few seconds, leaving nothing for the little birds but a taste of hungry.

Well, the Good Lord snatched up that pig again, and set him on that stump.

"Stay here!" He shouted. "You don't need another thing to eat! If you don't stop this greediness, I'm gonna have to make some changes in your situation, you hear?"

Pig said, "Yes, sir." He looked all pitiful and sorry, and the Good Lord walked away to try and feed those little birds again.

Pig's nose got there just as the corn and seeds and tidbits touched the ground. Sqwonk! Pig inhaled those good bits, and got snatched up again.

This time, when the Good Lord reached that tree stump, He set Himself down on it, with Pig on His lap. "Child," said the Good Lord, "you too greedy for your own good. I told you, if you kept up your greedy ways, I was gonna have to make a change in your situation, and I'm makin' it right now."

The Good Lord grabbed that long, long nose, and stretched it out as far as it would go. Woo, that hurt! Made Pig's eyes water, made him squeal, "Oink!"

Then the Good Lord squeezed that nose, and twisted and twisted until the thing snapped off, snap! Pig squealed, "Oink! Woo-eeee!"

Then, to add insult to injury, the Good Lord smacked what was left of Pig's nose and mashed it into that snuffling flat thing pigs wear on their faces to this very day.

Well, that hurt so bad, Pig's tail curled up. He couldn't squeal. He just grunted; he's been grunting and squealing ever since. And his tail stayed curled up, never straightened itself out again. Pig ran off to cool his aches in the very first puddle of mud.

That's how Pig learned to keep his nose out of other folks' business.

STORY NOTES

A lot of things happened "in the first days of Creation," an opening that let me know the story my grandfather or my father was about to tell wasn't in the Bible.

Daddy had a lot of these pourquoi tales. When I was little, I wondered if Daddy had been there in the first days of Creation, and managed to get aboard Noah's Ark. If he did, that meant that my mother was in the ark, too—folks got on board in pairs, you know.

Daddy seemed to know a lot about all the animals in those first days, so he had to be there. And he'd survived the flood. Sooo, which of Noah's sons was he, really? Then I figured it out. Noah's sons were Shem, Ham, and Japheth, and that last one was hard to pronounce. Now, my dad's nickname was "Jake," which sounded a bit like that unpronounceable name. Therefore ... Oh!

From then on, for me, the sons of Noah were Shem, Ham, and *Jake.* I never asked my father if that was true. Doing so would have broken a code of honor. It would have been like asking Clark Kent if he was Superman.

Papa Turtle and Monkey

Papa Turtle was a kind-hearted critter, a sweet ol' fella, always willing to help just about anybody. Folks knew him for his generous ways.

But, sometimes folks take advantage of a kind heart.

In the same neighborhood lived Monkey. Monkey had made himself known to everybody, too, but not by the same means as Papa Turtle. Monkey was known for causing trouble for some, and annoying many.

When Monkey asked for help, he never did anything in return. When he made a promise, he broke it with a laugh. He called stealing "borrowin'," and borrowin' was "keepin'."

Anybody with good sense called him a thief. But Monkey called himself "Smarter than Everybody".

You might know somebody like that.

On this particular day, Monkey was hungry, but he didn't want to cook, or hunt, or fish, or work, or shop. He just wanted to eat. And he knew nobody would ever think of inviting him for supper. But he also knew of somebody, a sweet and generous somebody, who kept a huge garden that might need some tending.

Papa Turtle loved to garden. Although he was built low to the ground, he was finding it harder and harder to get through the plowing and the planting and the watering and the weeding and the harvesting. But Papa Turtle had been helpful to so many folks, and generous with the goods from his harvests, so lots of critters offered to help him whenever they could. And Papa Turtle thanked them by giving them a portion of the bounty at harvest time, or a meal from his preserves and canned goods, which he would put up himself.

Monkey knew that, so he headed over to Papa Turtle's.

Now, everything was already planted and heartily growing. The weeds had already been pulled. The rains had tenderly watered the garden. There wasn't anything else to do and it wasn't yet time for harvest. But if Monkey offered to do some little thing for Papa Turtle, maybe he'd still get a free meal. Of course, he wouldn't really work, but he'd make it seem he was busy.

Monkey trotted on over to Papa Turtle's place, and said, "Good evenin', sir. I've come to help you with your work. Whatever you need done, I'll do. Just tell me what you need!"

Papa Turtle replied, "Well, thank you, young Monkey, but there's nothin' to do right now. And I'm just about ready to turn in for the night."

"Sir, ain't there anything you need done right now?" asked Monkey. "Please, I really, *really* want to help you."

Papa Turtle nodded his head a bit. Looked like he was having a tremendous think. "Well, maybe there is somethin' you can do for me, young Monkey," said Papa Turtle. "There's somethin' strange growin' on an odd tree in the woods behind my house, and I don't know what it is, but I think it might be good to eat. If you want, you can join me on my evenin' *perambulation*, and help me get what's growin' on that tree. I can't climb a tree, you know, never could. If you can bring down a big piece of that fruit, and it's good, I'll figger out how to fix it for us to eat."

Monkey had no idea what a "perambulation" was, but he figured he could ride it if Papa Turtle could. He'd do anything to get out of cooking his own meal. He was a bit perturbed when he realized a perambulation was a *walk* to inspect Papa Turtle's property and a longer *walk* down into the woods behind his house.

"There it is," Papa Turtle said when they got to a particular tree. It wasn't very big, but it was too tall for a turtle's arm to reach its fruit. And what fruit it was! It was long and almost egg-shaped, kind of dark yellowish-green turning brownish-black, strange and sweetly perfumed.

Monkey climbed up that little tree, grabbed a piece of fruit and squeezed it just a little to see if it was ripe. He wasn't sure what would happen. He wasn't sure if the thing was any good. But it squeezed open; inside were big brown seeds and sweet yellow pulp. Monkey tasted it. Ooo-ooo-ooo, it was good!

Papa Turtle shouted, "Monkey, what you think you're doin'? That fruit is on a tree in the woods on my property, which makes that my tree. I'll share with you; I'll give you some of that stuff. But don't eat it by yourself! Bring the fruit down and we'll share it."

Monkey said, "Sir, I was just tastin' it to see if it was ripe yet."

"Is it?" asked Papa Turtle.

"Not sure," said Monkey. "Better taste another one." He picked another piece of that wonderful stuff, squeezed it open, and started to eat.

"Wait!" yelled Papa Turtle. "Stop! Why you eatin' that one, too?"

"Hard to tell if these things are ripe," explained Monkey. "I better taste another one."

There were only seven pieces of fruit hangin' on that tree. Monkey ate all seven of them.

"Monkey, you ate all of those things!" cried Papa Turtle. "You just helpin' yourself to that fruit. I thought you wanted to help *me*!"

"I did," said Monkey, "I helped you figure out if those things were ripe. They were!"

"But we were supposed to share the fruit!" Papa Turtle fussed.

"We will!" Monkey yelled back at him. "I got my part.

Here's yours!"

Monkey threw the seeds from that fruit as hard as he could. Pim—pim—pim! The seeds bounced off poor Papa Turtle's shell and hit the ground. Monkey laughed and leaped from that little tree to a taller one, then to another tree, and another one, until he was far away from Papa Turtle and on his way home.

Well, that was the last straw for the animal community. When they heard what had happened to Papa Turtle, they went looking for Monkey. It was bad enough when Monkey was an annoyance for all of them, but it was a terrible thing for him to hurt Papa Turtle and cheat the poor ol' fella out of that fruit. Monkey heard folks fussing and muttering about him. He decided he'd better move someplace where folks didn't know him.

Monkey ran through the tops of the trees to a new neighborhood, full of all new folks.

But after a short while, he had annoyed those folks, too, and he had to move again.

Monkey was walking through the woods behind Papa Turtle's house. He smiled, remembering the trick he'd played on that poor ol' gentleman. Then he stopped. It was about the same time of year as when he'd taken that fruit from the strange little tree. And there, covering a large patch of ground, was a whole *slew* of those trees! The seeds he'd thrown at Papa Turtle had taken root, with a little help from Papa Turtle's green thumbs, and all those little trees were bearing fruit. That fruit smelled so good that Monkey invited himself to go get some.

When he started to climb the nearest tree, he heard Papa Turtle calling out to him, "Better not do that, Monkey!"

Monkey yelled back, "What you gonna do, Papa? You can't climb trees, remember? And you too slow to catch me when I come back down. What you got to stop me from doing what I want?"

Papa Turtle shouted, "I got friends!"

That's when Monkey felt a sting on his hand, then another sting on his other hand, then one on his foot, then one on his face. In no time at all, he was covered with bees. They buzzed,

ZZZZ ... Papa Turtle invited uzzzz to come live in
hizzzz treezzzz.
Our home izzzz safe here, and the fruit izzzz sweet,
and we guard hizzzz fruit and hizzzz home in return.
Go away, Monkey ... zzzzZZZZ!

Stubborn Monkey kept climbing, getting stung more and more. He yelled, "Ow! You can't stop me with a sting or two! I've got ... tenacity! I'll get that fruit, and get your honey, too! OW!"

Then he felt something grab his tail. He looked down, and saw a long black snake holding on to his tail, stretching it and pulling it, and sliding around the tree trunk.

SSSStop, foolish creature," hissed the snake.
I work for Papa Turtle, too.
He ssssaved me from frightened
two-legged crittersss who would've killed me,
and I protect hisss treessss. Go away!

Monkey wouldn't go, but he couldn't argue anymore. Even his tongue was stung. All he could say was, "Ooo-ooo-ooo-ah-ah-AH-EEE!" That's what some monkeys say even now.

Monkey couldn't even scream when the snake yanked him off the tree. Snake lifted him up by his tail, and swung him around and around, shaking off all the bees with that dizzy move. Then Snake threw Monkey clean out of the woods. That swinging and throwing stretched Monkey's tail into the long tail he and some of his kin wear today.

Monkey left that place and never came back. And Papa Turtle's trees grew. Whenever the fruit was just right, Papa Turtle shared it with everybody.

His trees still grow, if the bigger trees and the critters protect them. Some folks call their fruit West Virginia Bananas. Other folks say they're named after Papa Turtle. They call the fruit and the trees Paw-paws, to honor a sweet and generous ol' fella.

STORY NOTES

The pawpaw is a medium-sized tree that seems to need the canopy of larger trees to block out sunlight and help it thrive. Too much sunlight seems to keep it from growing; when the larger trees are cut, the paw-paws don't seem to "come back"—survive. It grows throughout the Appalachian region, and bears the largest native fruit in North America. The fruit tends to be a rich black color when it is ripe. But, it is also known as the West Virginia Banana—a misnomer, for it is not of the banana family—and I remember seeing it in its unripe, greenish state.

The flavor is tropical, kind of a mango-banana mix, and delicious. Research has found that the paw-paw is a good source of nutrients and anti-oxidants. Go to www.pawpaw.kysu.edu/ for more information on that. Or plan on attending Southern Ohio's annual Ohio Pawpaw Festival (http://www.ohiopawpawfest.com/).

I don't know that there is an agreed-upon way to write "pawpaw." We always used a hyphen between the syllables, but I've seen it as two words, or as one two-syllable word with no hyphen; I've also seen both syllables capitalized, and separated by hyphens as if to give the name more distinction and class. Merriam-Webster.com prefers one two-syllable word with no hyphen.

Who cares? The paw-paw season is short. If you can find 'em, get some and enjoy the gift from Papa Turtle's green thumbs.

Rabbit and Fox at the Well

Rabbit was running this way and that way, zigzagging across the meadow to get away from Fox. He'd always been able to stay ahead of Fox, but this time, that red-tailed varmint was catching up.

Rabbit kept a-zigging and a-zagging, a-hopping and a-hurrying, and, pretty soon, he heard Fox a-puffing and a-panting. That made Rabbit laugh as he ran, ha! He got a bit too biggedy about his running, and the next thing he knew, Zhwoop!

Rabbit had fallen into a well dug in the ground, and landed in the bucket. Fox heard him hit that metal, heard him yell, "Ow!" Down, down, down Rabbit went, until the bucket landed, plop, in the well water. And the other bucket attached to the same rope went up, up, up. Rabbit had fallen into trouble. Now, how in the world was he gonna get back out?

Up above, still puffing and panting, Fox started to laugh, "Ah-ha-ahahaha—cough, cough—you caught yourself this time, Rabbit! What you gonna do now?"

"What do you mean, what am I gonna do now?" Rabbit asked. "can't you see what I'm doin'?"

"No," Fox panted, "It's ... too ... dark down there. I can't see a thing ....

"But I can hear you, and I know you are one trapped

Rabbit! Ha-ah-ha—cough, cough—trapped!"

That's all Rabbit needed to know. Fox couldn't see the bottom of the well. Rabbit could tell him anything. And he did.

"Oh, this don't feel like a trap, friend Fox," Rabbit boasted. "This feels like a trip to fishin' paradise. Why there are fish swimmin' all around down here, and they are already seasoned and fried up and ready to eat! Oh, I wish you could taste these fish!" Rabbit made a few munching and swallowing sounds, and then he burped, "Ur-up! Oh, I better slow down. But these fish taste so good!"

Well, the whole point of Fox's chasing Rabbit was the procurement of his supper. His stomach growled at the thought of already-fried fish.

"Rabbit, are those fish hot?" asked Fox.

"Just the right heat for meltin' in your mouth, Fox," said Rabbit. He munched and swallowed loudly, and added a few "Yummm" and "Mm-m-M" exclamations.

"Are those fish wearin' corn meal, or flour? I like my fish rolled in corn meal, yellow corn meal, to be exact," said Fox.

"Well, that's what they wearin'!" hollered Rabbit. "Fried up just right, and you should taste the pepper and the salt on these things!

"Oh, you can't," Rabbit went on, "'Cause you're up there, and the fish are down here. Too bad for you, Fox."

"Too bad, my foot!" spouted Fox. "There's a bucket up here, hangin' from the same rope that's tied to yours. I'm gonna jump in this one, and come down there and get some fish. And when I'm finished eatin' that fish, I'm gonna come up and get you, and make myself some rabbit stew!"

Fox jumped in that bucket, and down, down, down he went. Which meant Rabbit went up, up, up. When Rabbit reached the top of the well, he hopped out of that bucket. Poor Fox floated in the bucket at the bottom of the well. Fox's bucket wibbled and wobbled and bobbed in the water, until Fox was too afraid to yell for help.

Rabbit went on to the nearest garden, where he pulled up some carrots and cabbage for his supper. Fox didn't see daylight until the farmer came to get a cool drink from that bucket.

I don't know what the farmer thought when he pulled up a bucket of Fox instead of water.

I do know Fox stayed in the bucket long enough to say, "Thank you!" Then he leaped out and went on home. He was so glad to feel the earth beneath his feet that he forgot about supper. He went to bed that night, and dreamed of fried fish.

STORY NOTES

You can find a variant of this story in *Uncle Remus: His Songs and Sayings*[1]. Its title is "Old Mr. Rabbit, He's a Good Fisherman." That version has all the animals working together in the garden, and Rabbit complaining of a briar in his hand, when his real problem is the need for a nice, cool place to take a nap. The bucket at the well seems like a good place to rest, but gravity pulls Rabbit's plans for a nap into a dark adventure.

I liked Daddy's way of telling it better. To me, Rabbit seemed too smart to try and take a nap in a bucket that would drop into a well. But he might fall into the bucket. Accidents do happen, even to the smartest of us.

Now, about those fried fish. Well, in our family, Pop-pops caught 'em and Grandma Jo or Mama or Aunt Kat or Aunt Freda fried 'em, coated in a batter of yellow cornmeal, pepper, and salt. Then she served them on a big platter with greens or cole slaw and corn bread or hush puppies.

Is your mouth waterin' yet?

1. Joel Chandler Harris, *Uncle Remus: His Songs and Sayings.*(New York: D. Appleton & Company, 1880).

Rabbit and Lion at the Well

What do you do when somebody is threatening to turn your grandma into a midnight snack? Well, if you're Rabbit, you don't sit around and cry about it. You don't hide, or run away. You start using your head for more than a place to hang your ears, and you come up with a plan to save your grandma.

That's what Rabbit had to do. He had to think of a way to save his grandma from Young Mean Lion that had moved into a cave near Animal Town. That young fella was meaner than old Boss Lion could ever be, so mean he'd scared Boss Lion away. Old Boss Lion took his family for a long vacation to Florida and he never came back.

Soon, the folks in Animal Town grew nostalgic for Old Boss Lion. Sure, he ate somebody every now and again, but it was usually someone nobody knew. Being politically aware, Old Boss Lion used to send his wife to hunt far away from his own community. She'd bring back strangers, usually mean and ornery ones, and roast up a fine meal for Boss Lion.

Young Mean Lion started to prowl the town each and every day.

He seemed hungry *all the time*. Young Mean Lion didn't care if folks got upset when he gulped down a neighbor. Young Mean Lion would knock on any neighbor's door, swallow some good and kind body as soon as the door was opened, then head on home without even offering an apology.

Folks in Animal Town began taking it personally.

Too many neighbors were getting swallowed.

Animal Town folks became afraid to open their doors. Locked inside all the time, folks were getting hungry themselves. Some folks were missing family members. Folks were crying a whole lot, moaning and sulking. There was a spirit of sadness in Animal Town.

Seemed like folks should, at the very least, feel safe in their homes. Seemed like they should be able to walk out of their houses and find a meal for their kinfolk. Seemed like Rabbit's grandma ought to be able to visit her neighbors and work in her garden. Rabbit decided he had to do something about that young lion. And of course, in the time it takes to wiggle his nose, Rabbit had a plan to make the community a safe place for his grandma, and everybody else.

Young Mean Lion's cave was beyond the well at the edge of the holler. That evening, Rabbit walked right up to the mouth of the cave. Since it didn't have a door, Rabbit hollered, "Knock, knock!"

Young Mean Lion growled, "Who's there?"

Rabbit said, "May."

Young Mean Lion snarled, "May who?"

Rabbit shouted, "May-be you better stop knockin' on doors and eatin' up my neighbors!"

Well, Young Mean Lion didn't think that was funny. He ran out the cave and shoved Rabbit to the ground. He pressed his big paws down on Rabbit's chest. He breathed in a double lung-full and exhaled his Mean Lion breath right into Rabbit's face. That young lion's breath smelled a bit like Mrs. Squirrel used to smell ... uh, oh. Another neighbor gone.

"You got some nerve, Rabbit," growled Young Mean Lion, "comin' here disturbin' my nap. And *now* I'm hungry. Rrrrrrr ... since you're here, maybe I will just eat *you*!"

Rabbit pushed Young Mean Lion's paws off his chest. He jumped up, but he didn't run. He dusted himself off, straightened out his ears, and said, "Maybe you should just *listen* first. Iiiiiiiiii have a plan."

"A plan? A plan for what?" asked Young Mean Lion. "Don't make me wait for my meal. I'll get even hungrier, and have to fill my stomach with somebody besides you. And I don't feel like huntin'."

"Why, that's the plan, Brother Lion," said Rabbit. "I have figured out a way to keep you from waiting for any meal. And you won't have to hunt for your meals anymore, either. Back in Animal Town, all the neighbors will gather together once every day, real early, maybe sunrise. We'll draw straws that I'll pull from my own hearth broom. Whoever gets the shortest straw will just come on out here to your cave and jump into your skillet. Then we'll draw for the next shortest straw, and the next, until we've figgered out the menu for your day. And we'll do that every day. That way, we won't have to worry about you comin' into town, scarin' folks and eatin' 'em. And you won't have to do any huntin'."

This sounded good to Young Mean Lion, too good to pass up. Without another thought, he told Rabbit he would need five meals a day, every day: a big breakfast, a touch of brunch, a grand supper, a sun-goes-down dinner, and a sweet, tender dessert.

Now, anybody who knows lions knows that wasn't true. Young Mean Lion didn't need that much food. He didn't even need to eat every day. That young lion was just being greedy. But Rabbit agreed to the menu.

"Well, that's fine. That's settled then," Rabbit said. "I'll just go tell the other critters and get my broom, and come breakfast-time you will get your first new victim."

Young Mean Lion roared, "Awwrrr, breakfast better get here at sunrise, or I'll be at *your* door tomorrow, Rabbit!"

Rabbit ran off.

Young Mean Lion sat at the door of his cave. His mouth was grinning and watering at the same time as he thought about all the good meals that would be coming his way. He wouldn't have to hunt; he wouldn't even have to walk into town. He'd be able to sleep as much as he wanted. He'd never have to worry about …

"Ow, Lion, ow, Lion!" Rabbit interrupted Young Mean Lion's daydream. Rabbit was running as if he was in a race, with his ears perked up straight to listen for danger. His eyes were as wide open as a rabbit's eyes could be, and his mouth was stretched wide open as he yelled, "Oh, Lion, ow!"

Rabbit ran right up and over Young Mean Lion's nose, over his mane, and down his back. Rabbit hugged Lion's leg as if it was his mama. "Help me, Brother Lion, help me! Old Boss Lion is gonna eat me!"

Young Mean Lion peeled Rabbit off his back leg, and held him up by his ears. "Rrrrrrr, What Old Boss Lion? I thought he moved to Florida." he growled.

"I met him at the well just down the path," Rabbit whimpered. "He wouldn't let me go back to town, said I was his dessert tonight. He yanked my ears and nibbled on my toenails. He's as mean as a *wampus cat*! I had to beg for my life!

"I told him I was workin' for you, and that I had to get that plan in order for your meals. I had to tell him the plan, or he would have thrown me right down his nasty throat.

"Then he told me I was gonna work for *him*, send the critters to *him*, or I was gonna be *his* next meal. Old Boss Lion told me to come back here and tell you that. He said there was nothin' you could do about it. Ow, he scared me! Why, Brother Lion, he's even scarier than *you*!"

"Rrrrrr, awrrr, take me to this Old Boss Lion!" snarled Young Mean Lion. "I'll take care of him!"

Rabbit pushed Young Mean Lion in front of him. With a trembling tongue and nervous little whimpers, Rabbit told Young Mean Lion which way to turn on the path.

They saw the well, but they didn't see Old Boss Lion. Rabbit tiptoed around, peeking under the berry bushes, poking his head quickly behind the trees, standing on tippy-toes to look in the well …

Then he gasped and dropped to the ground. "Sh, Brother Lion," Rabbit whispered, "Old Boss Lion is *in* the well!"

Young Mean Lion strutted to the well. He shook his mane so that he'd look bigger and more powerful. Then he stood on his hind legs, pressed his paws on the edges of the well so that his claws showed, stuck his head into the well, and roared, "AAAAWWWRRRR! I am the king of the forest!"

And the lion in the well roared back, "AAAWWWRRRR! I am the king of the forest!"

Well, that was a surprise.

Young Mean Lion stepped back, looking a bit confused. That Old Boss Lion didn't seem to be afraid of him.

"Don't let that old fella get away with that, Brother Lion," Rabbit said. He pushed Young Mean Lion back toward the well. "You best give Old Boss Lion what for, or you won't be the big man around here. The plan for your daily meals will never happen. Why, he'll take your food before it can get to you. Go on, give him what for!"

Young Mean Lion sidled up to the well, pushed himself back up so his claws sparkled in the sunlight. Wearing his meanest glare, Young Mean Lion looked into the well. That other, older lion glared back at him. He sure looked mean. In fact, he didn't even look *so old.*

"You don't know who you're messin' with, Rrrrrr," Young Mean Lion growled.

And the lion in the well growled, "You don't know who you're messin' with, Rrrrrr."

"Keep playin' with me, and I'll tear off your ears, lion!" Young Mean Lion showed all his teeth.

That lion in the well showed all *his teeth,* too, and threatened, "Keep playin' with me, and I'll tear off your ears, lion!"

Young Mean Lion glared even harder as he yelled, "I-I'm gonna beat the wampus cat right outta you!"

The lion in the well glared even harder and yelled, "I-I'm

gonna beat the wampus cat right outta you!"

"I dare you!" shouted Young Mean Lion. He heard, "I dare you!" shouted right back at him.

Young Mean Lion roared. He snarled.

He shook his mane. Young Mean Lion leaped at that old lion … who roared, snarled, shook his mane, leaped, and …

SPLASH!

After a whole lot of thrashing and gulping, both lions were gone.

"Hmph," said Rabbit, "that's too bad. In fact, that's terrible. Now we're gonna have to dig another well."

Then Rabbit went on home, and told his grandma and the neighbors that they were safe. He claimed the Young Mean Lion had left the neighborhood for good. He claimed that he had seen to it that the critter would never come their way again.

I'm not saying that the folks in Animal Town believed him, but they were grateful when their friends and neighbors didn't disappear anymore.

Rabbit warned folks that the water smelled funny in the well that was near Lion's abandoned cave. Folks wondered how Rabbit knew the water was tainted and that they'd have to dig another well. But they agreed that there was an odd odor rising up from that old well. They filled it with dirt, covered it with wood planks, and started a new one. Rabbit didn't help with the work. Rabbit never helped with much of anything … or so folks thought.

Rabbit's grandma never had a doubt that Rabbit had gotten rid of that Young Mean Lion. She didn't care how. She made Rabbit a carrot cake as big as a wagon wheel. And Rabbit ate the whole thing all by himself.

🌿 🌿

STORY NOTES

Let's talk about that wampus cat. In folklore, the cat was said to have once been a beautiful woman who didn't trust her husband. It's said she wondered what he did when he went off with the other men. One night, wrapped in the skin of a wild cat, she followed him to the place where only the men could gather for stories and ritual. When the men discovered her watching their ceremonies, the woman was taken before the male elder (or medicine man, depending on who is telling the story, I guess) and changed into a creature forever wrapped in the skin she'd used to cover herself. The woman was now half-woman and half-cat. From that day on, she was said to be all meanness and madness and terrifying howls.

Forever after, like the call of a banshee, her cry predicted death.

The wampus cat's story originated among the Cherokee, but pioneers and frontier folk carried it across the country from the Appalachian region to Texas and beyond. The wampus cat has become the mascot for several high school sports teams, in Arkansas, Louisiana, Oklahoma, Texas, and Tennessee.

We had "*wampus*" temperaments and reactions in my family—you might call them temper tantrums—but we didn't have specific wampus cat stories. I also recall Daddy saying, as he watched a boxer "beat the tar out of" someone, "He knocked the wampus outta him!" Beating the tar out of someone and knocking the wampus out of him or her seemed to have the same meaning: somebody got "whupped". Another phrase that my mother and my father used was "knocking the walk-about hockey" out of someone.

Disgusting imagery.

I don't know where a body would store walk-about hockey. And I don't want to know. The language is colorful enough to make the meaning quite clear.

We had anecdotes about other strange things, boo-daddies and boo-mamas, even boo-babies, and other "thangs" that I've forgotten, but I never heard the story of the wampus cat until I was grown and traveling to tell stories. An older gentleman at the Haunting in the Hills Storytelling Festival at Big South Fork National Park in Tennessee asked me if I

knew stories about the wampus cat. When I said no, he asked, "You sure
knew stories about the wampus cat. When I said no, he asked, "You sure
yer from Appalachia? *Everybody* knows the wampus cat!"

He didn't give me his name, but he did give me the information I've
just passed on to you. And he said, "You need to write that down." So
I just did.

My maternal grandmother, Jean Wilson Arkward. She died when I was very young, but I remember her.

My mother, Jean Elizabeth Arkward Cooper Matthews

My Dad, Edward Maclin Cooper

This my grandfather, "Pop-Pop" Byard WIlmer Arkward,
and his father, my "Great-Pop", Jerome Arkward.

My Dad, Edward Maclin Cooper, on Aunt Kat's back porch

My sister, Kimmy, and me

FOLKS

The first story in this section, "Clever Jackie," is one of my favorite "fool" tales. It begins where most human insecurities live: within the homebound child or provisionary adult mentality.

The second, "Josephus," is a story that remains very close to my heart, because the title character seems willing to believe what someone else—a person in authority—tells him about himself; in reality, Josephus knows his own strengths and capabilities. "Josephus" introduces four tales in which I've concentrated on one very special character, John, a fictional protagonist whose stories speak to the intelligence, creativity, and survival skills of those rebelling against captivity prior to Emancipation.

The last of the stories about the everyman named John is a good lead-in for the next section, "Spookers & Haints."

Clever Jackie

Jack was running around in his front yard, running in circles, faster and faster, until he got so dizzy that he ran right into the big oak tree.

BAM!

Jack's mama heard the noise, and came running outside. There was Jack, picking himself up off the ground, rubbing his forehead, and laughing, "Ah ha, ah ha, ha, ow, Mama, I ran into that tree! Look at my head! I got a big ol' knot this time, ow! Ah ha, ha, ha!"

Mama said, "Jack, you gotta stop runnin' like that. Bashin' into trees can't be good for your brain."

Jack said, "Yes, ma'am, I'll stop runnin' into the tree. I'll go in the backyard, and help Daddy cut the firewood."

"No!" Mama shouted. "Don't want you near any sharp tools, child. You jus' stay here in the front yard."

But Jack didn't know what to do. If he couldn't run around in circles, what was there to do?

Jack started jumping up and down as hard and as high as he could. Next thing he knew, BAM! He'd bashed his head on an oak tree branch, and landed hard on the ground.

"Ow!" Jack yelled as he rubbed his backside. "I almost

broke my *cushions* that time, ah ha, ha, ha!"

Jack's Mama was watching him through the kitchen window. As she stirred up supper, a meaty *slumgullion*, she saw him jump up, bash his head, fall down, and bash his backside. Mama came running. From the porch, she saw Jack getting up off the ground, limping a bit, and laughing.

Mama shook her head, "Jack, whatever you were doin' out here, stop. Just stand still."

Jack tried standing still, but it was such a difficult thing to do.

After a while, Jack hollered, "Mama, this is boring! Can't I do something else?"

Mama hollered from the kitchen window, "Well, while you're standin' there, you could make up a song. Find a tune in your head. Make up some words to fit the tune. Make the words rhyme. Why, if you can do all of that, Jack, I know that someday you will be a clever boy."

Well, Jack stood there straining his brain to come up with a tune. Thinking made his eyes water and his hair hurt. But after a while, he'd come up with something that sounded good:

My mama calls me Clever Jackie, even though I'm wacky.
I'm learnin' everything I can so someday I can say,
My mama calls me Clever Jackie, even though I'm wacky.
I'm learnin' everything I can so someday I can say,
My mama ...

Jack's mama hollered, "Jackie! Stop singin' that song! Why do you keep goin' on and on and on with it?"

"Song's got a good beginnin', Mama," said Jack, "and it's got a pretty good middle. Song don't have an endin' yet, see?

My mama calls me ...

"Never mind!" Mama shouted. "Come on in and get a bite to eat. Your daddy and I have to tell you somethin' about what you're gonna do tomorrow."

Jack said, "Yes, ma'am." He wasn't really bright, but he was always polite.

Jack, his mama and Daddy had a fine supper, that meaty slumgullion with *corn cake*. Then Mama and Daddy told Jack what he would be doing the next day.

"You're gonna make your way through our woods and over to your aunty and uncle's farm, to help them with the work over there. You be helpful and you work the very best that you can. You're gonna stay with them until that work is done.

"Times are hard," Jack's Daddy went on, "and folks are poor. We don't have much, can't afford to hire on extra hands, so we help each other as much as we can. But you know your aunty and uncle are gonna want to give you somethin' for your work."

Jack's mama added quickly, "Whatever they give you, Jack, you remember to say thank you. Then you come on home, you hear?"

Jack said, "Yes, sir. Yes, ma'am." He wasn't really bright, but he was always polite.

The next morning found Jack making his way through the words, and still working on that song. He wasn't finished with it yet. It went on and on and on ...

When he got to his aunty and uncle's house, they were waiting at the back door to greet him. But his aunty asked, "Jack what was that noise we heard comin' through the woods?"

"Me!" Jack said proudly. "I'm workin' on a song. It's got a good beginnin', got a middle. Doesn't have an endin' yet, listen:"

My mama ...

"No! Don't sing it anymore!" Jack's uncle winced and frowned. But then he smiled. "Come on in the house, child. We're not gonna get on that work yet. Today we're just gonna talk and tell stories, maybe sing, but not *that* song! Then we'll have a fine supper, do some chores, have a little dinner, get ready for bed, and get to work in the mornin'."

And that's what they did.

The next morning, Jack got up early. And he worked so hard that all the work that needed to be done was done in just three days.

His aunty was pleased. His uncle was proud. They wanted to give him something.

"Here," said Jack's aunty. "Here's my best sewing needle for you."

Jack couldn't believe it! "I worked for three days, and all I get is a ... oops...thank you," Jack said to be polite.

"Jack, that's more than just a sewing needle," said his aunty. "That needle is made of pure silver. It's been passed down to the young women in the family for generations. You're the first young man to even touch it, Jack! And I want to give you somethin' else ..."

Jack's aunty reached into her apron pocket, and pulled out a large spool of white thread.

"I make this thread myself," she said. "I card the wool and spin the thread until it's fine and silky. And I don't want you to lose that needle, so I'm gonna tie it onto the thread, and knot it good and tight. Here, Jack, my silky thread and the silver needle for you."

Jack took these small treasures, one in each hand, and held them high as he headed for the woods. "Thank you!" he called back to his aunty and uncle. He wasn't really bright, but he was always polite.

Jack traipsed carefully and quietly through the woods. He held that thread and needle high, so he could keep an eye on both and not lose them. But his fingers started to tingle, and his hands fell asleep. When the tingling feeling started to creep down his arms, Jack decided he needed to do something about it.

He looked at the spool of thread. The ends looked like

wheels. Jack figured that spool could roll along behind him; he threw it over his shoulder. Now you know the spool didn't roll. It lay where it was dropped, and bounced a bit as the thread unwound. The thread unwound all the way down the path through the forest, but Jack never looked behind him.

One arm was down and the blood was circulating. But the other one was going to sleep. Jack figured the needle was attached to the thread, and the thread was wound around the spool. If he draped the threaded needle over himself in some way, he wouldn't have to carry it. So Jack threw the needle up and over his shoulder.

Well, that needle started swinging and sliding down Jack's back, down and down, until it poked him in a most inappropriate place. Ow!

But Jack wasn't clever enough to pull it back up and over his shoulder. No, he just kept on walking home with that thing jabbing him in his ... cushions.

When Jack got home, he knocked on the door. He always did, even though it was his home, so that he could announce himself to his mother. This time, when she opened the door, Jack said more than, "Mama, I'm home."

He added, "Aunty gave me her silver sewing needle." He reached around. "Mpf, ow! Here it is," he said as he pulled it from the place where it had stuck.

"And she gave me a spool of silky, shiny ... thread?" Jack was finally looking behind himself. He saw a trail of white thread leading back into the woods.

"Oh, Jack," said his mama as she took the needle from his hand. "Your aunty makes that thread to make a little more money for the family. She uses it in all her quilting, and she sells it for a good price. Maybe I can roll it back up, but it's gonna be all dirty. Well, at least you didn't lose the needle."

Jack's mama bit the knot off the thread and put the needle safely into her apron pocket. Then she folded her arms and looked at Jack.

"Jack, a few weeks from now," she said, "you're gonna be goin' back over to you aunty and uncle's house. You're gonna help them with their farmin' again. And they're gonna want to pay you somethin'."

"You remember to say thank-you, but, whatever it is, don't do what you did with the needle and thread. You take whatever they give you and put it in your shirt pocket. Then you come on home, you hear?"

Jack rubbed his cushions and said, "Yes, ma'am." He wasn't really bright, but he was always polite.

Two weeks later, Jack was making his way through the woods. He was still working on that song. It went on and on and on ...

When he got to his aunty and uncle's house, they were standing at the back door. He wasn't sure if they were glad to see him. They didn't seem to be smiling.

His aunty asked, "Jack, that song of yours scared the birds outta the trees. We could tell where you were walkin'. Child, do you know another song?"

"Not yet," said Jack. "I'm still workin' on that one. It ain't finished yet, see:"

My mama ...."

"No! Don't sing!" Jack's aunty and uncle both winced and frowned. But then his uncle said, "Come on in the house, child. We're not gonna work yet. We're just gonna talk and tell stories, maybe sing, but not *that* song! Then we'll have a fine supper, do some chores, have a little dinner, get ready for bed, and get to work in the mornin'."

And that's what they did.

The next morning, Jack got up early. He worked so hard that all the work was done in just two days.

His aunty was pleased. His uncle was proud. They wanted to give him something.

Jack," said his uncle, "I know your aunty gave you a family heirloom last time you were here. I want to give you another one."

"Oh, no, not another needle ... oops ... thank you," said Jack.

"No, not another needle." Jack's uncle glared at him a bit. Then he handed Jack a long, beautiful walking stick. The wood was smooth, polished to a high sheen, and the shaft was decorated with carved flowers and leafy vines.

"That was your great-great-granddaddy's walking stick," said Jack's uncle. "He found a branch lyin' on the ground in those woods when he was a boy. He took it home, and removed the bark, and did all the carvin' himself. It's a real treasure, Jack, and, even though you don't need a cane now, I'm passin' it on to you."

Jack gently rubbed the wood, and admired the fine craftsmanship of his great-great-granddaddy. "Thank you," he said as he headed for the woods. He wasn't really bright, but he was always polite.

Jack carried that long walking stick with reverence. Then he remembered what his mama had told him, and he shoved the walking stick into his shirt pocket.

All the way through the woods, that thing kept bobbing around and whacking Jack in the head. But he wasn't clever enough to pull it out of that pocket and carry it. He just kept walking and getting whacked in the head.

When he got home, Jack knocked on the door, but he didn't announce himself. His mama opened it, and screamed, "Jack! What happened to your head?!?"

Jack whimpered, "Mama, they gave me great-great-granddaddy's walking stick ...." He held it out to his mother, " ... and it hurt real bad."

Jack's mama set the cane inside the door. Then she got some cold water from the well, dipped a rag in the bucket, and slapped the rag on Jack's bumped-up head. She sighed, "Oh, Jack, that wasn't very clever."

She sighed again, "Jack, in a couple weeks or so, you're gonna go over and help your aunty and uncle again. And they're gonna want to pay you somethin'. Whatever it is, you accept it. But don't put it in your shirt pocket. Maybe, if you carry it over your shoulders, you'll be safer.

"Remember to say thank-you, Jack. And, whatever they give you this time, just throw it over your shoulders, you hear?"

Jack held the cold rag against his head. "Yes, ma'am, Mama," he said. He wasn't really bright, but he was always polite.

Three weeks later, Jack was making his way through the woods again. And, yes, he was still working on that song. It went on and on and on ...

Nobody was at the door when Jack got to his aunty and uncle's house. But the family dog was trembling and hiding under the front porch. The hens were squawking and laying eggs all over the yard. The cows were standing, one on top of the other, in a corner of the barn. And Jack could hear his uncle yelling from somewhere, "Boy, don't sing that song anymore. You are driving us all out of our minds!"

"Yes, sir!" Jack yelled back. He walked into the house and found his aunty flat on her back and crying on the settee in the parlor, "He's singin' that song again! Make him stop! Make him stop!"

"I stopped! Sorry, ma'am!" Jack didn't know what else to say. He wasn't really bright, but he was always polite.

Well, there wasn't much talking that afternoon. No stories, no songs. But they had a good dinner, and went to bed early, so they would be ready to work in the morning.

The next morning, Jack got up before sunrise. He worked so hard that all the work was done in just one day.

His aunty was pleased. His uncle was proud. They wanted to give him something.

His uncle handed him a rope.

"Jack, you are a hard-workin' boy, and we're real happy with the way you work," said his uncle. "I wanted to give you somethin' real special. My favorite horse had a foal. And that foal is now a filly big enough for you to ride. You can teach her how to pull a wagon. In a year or so, you could ride her in one of those big races, maybe make a little more money. Here, Jack, a fine little filly for you."

Jack took the rope from his uncle's hands and petted his new treasure. "A horse? For me? Thank you!" he grinned.

He wasn't really bright, but he was always polite.

Jack was leading his horse back through the woods to his home, when he remembered what his mama had told him. So he dropped the rope, got his arms underneath that filly, and he lifted her up onto his shoulders.

It wasn't easy, and it wasn't comfortable, and it truly wasn't fun. That filly had more sense than Jack. She knew she wasn't supposed to be up there on his shoulders. She kicked Jack in the chest, and the shoulders, on his back, and on his head. But Jack just kept walking through the woods.

A little bit later, Jack's mama heard somebody kicking the door. She swung it open, ready to fuss at her child, but … "Jack!"

Jack couldn't announce himself. All he could say was, "Mama … get this … horse off … o' me!"

Mama pushed Jack down to his knees, so that filly could jump off his back. She and Jack's daddy let that poor horse run around the yard and stretch her legs, while Mama got cool water from the well, dipped a bunch of rags into the bucket, and slapped them all over Jack to try and get the lumps and bumps and bruises and knots to stop swelling.

As Daddy led the filly to the barn, to give her some water and a little something to eat, Mama moaned, "Oh, Jack …."

She shook her head and patted her chest, as if she were about to get the vapors. "Jack, I'm almost afraid to tell you this," she said, and Mama began to cry.

"In three weeks time, you're supposed to go over and help your aunty and uncle with their work again. And they're gonna want to give you somethin' … and I'm afraid that … whatever they give you … might kill you, child!"

Jack's mama bawled a while, then calmed herself. "Jack," she continued, "whatever they give you, you remember to say thank-you. But, if it's as big as what was just runnin' around the yard, honey, just ride it home, you hear?"

Jack rubbed the lumps and bumps and bruises and knots. "Yes, ma'am," he said. He wasn't really bright, but he was always polite.

Three weeks later, there was Jack, running through the woods and working on that song as loudly as he could. It went on and on and on ...

The cows were pitifully mooing, the hens were squawking, the dog was whining, all somewhere Jack couldn't see. And nobody was at the door when Jack got to his aunty and uncle's house. But he could hear someone in their kitchen. So he walked in, and politely called out, "Hello?"

There was his aunty. Her eyeballs were twitching. Her hair was standing on end. She was trembling and shaking as she clutched an upside-down broom and screamed, "Just ... let me ... git him ... one time!"

Jack's uncle was holding her back, and shouting, "No! No! No!" Then he snatched the broom and yelled, "Let ME do it!"

Jack knew he'd done to his aunty and uncle the same thing that he often did to his mama and Daddy. He'd somehow danced on the last nerve each one had, until it snapped.

"Sorry, sir! Sorry, Ma'am!" he cried. He wasn't really bright, but he was always, always polite.

Jack's uncle breathed slowly, and seemed to relax. He set the broom down by the door, and patted Jack's shoulder. But he was twitching and trembling just like Jack's aunty as he stammered, "D-d-do NOT sing that song ANYMORE! Eat—sleep—w-w-work in the morning!"

And that's what they did.

The next morning, Jack got up early. He worked so hard that all the work was done in just a half a day.

His aunty was pleased. His uncle was proud. They wanted to give him something.

With a smile of satisfaction, Jack's aunty handed him another rope. "Jack," she grinned, "we truly are proud of the way you work. Honey, you work so hard! And now, I'd like to give you something that's sure to help you make a little money for yourself."

"She is one of my favorites. You can milk her, and keep or sell the milk, or make cheese from it, and sell what you don't want or need. I'll bring over her calf for you. If you take good care of them, I'll help you get your own herd started, so you can make more money for yourself and the family."

"Here, Jack," his aunty said, "One of my favorite cows for you."

Jack took that rope, looked at that grand cow, and said, "Thank you!" He wasn't really bright, but he was always polite.

Jack had led the cow into the woods before he remembered what his mama had told him. If his aunty and uncle gave him something as big as what was running around the yard ...

Jack dropped the rope. He swung himself up onto that cow. "Okay, cow," Jack said, with a big grin making his face shine like sunlight. "Let's go ... uh ... uh oh ... cow where'd your head go? Oh, no, cow! Your head is gone! How did your tail get where your head is supposed to be?"

Jack frantically looked around, to the left and the right, on the ground to his front, to his back ... "Oh," laughed Jack, "Ah ha, ah ha, ha! There it is!"

Yep, Jack was sitting backwards on that cow. But he wasn't clever enough to turn around. Still, he didn't want to fall off. No, that wouldn't be clever at all. So Jack tightly grabbed the cow's tail, yoink!

Cow said, "Moo?"

"Come on, cow, giddy-up, go!" Jack commanded. But the cow didn't go. To make it move, Jack pulled the cow's tail, yoink!

Cow said, "Moo!" She started trotting through the woods. That trot was enough to bounce Jack this way, and that way, and every which-a-way. And Jack got nervous, wanted the cow to stop. So he pulled her tail, yoink!

Cow said, "*Moo!*" She started running. And Jack bounced this way and that way, and every which-a-way. He wanted that cow to stop. So he pulled her tail again, and harder, *yoink!*

Cow said, "MOO-OO!" She started running like her tail had caught fire. And Jack bounced this way, and that way, and this way, and that way, and every which-away. The next thing he knew, Jack was airborne. He yelled and laughed, "AHHH, ah HA, AH HA, Ahhhh!!!" Finally, he landed, BAM!

"Ow," Jack whimpered, "m-m-my cushions ..."

That poor cow was terrified! She just kept on running, until she ran right into the door of Jack's family's house, BAM!

Mama thought someone had knocked on the door. It was a loud knock, couldn't be her son. Mama called out cautiously, "Who is it?"

Cow said, "Moo."

Mama opened the door to find a very confused-looking cow staring at her. And behind the cow, limping and sniffling came Jack.

Mama sighed, "Ohhh, Jack ...

"Your daddy and I have talked about this. You can get yourself over to your aunty and uncle's, but you can't get back home without halfway killin' yourself! We decided that if there was trouble this time, we'd have to make a change in things. And it looks like there was trouble."

Mama hugged her son as he rubbed his cushions. "From now on, your daddy and I will go over with you, stay and help on your aunty and uncle's farm, and bring you back home. And if there's extra work to be done over here, they'll come on over and help us here. But we'll be with you on the to and from journeys, until you are more clever, you hear?"

Jack said, "Yes, ma'am." He wasn't really bright, but he was always ... well, you know.

And he did grow up to be clever. Jack learned to use that silver needle and silky thread to make a quilt as fine as his aunty's quilts. He learned to choose branches fallen from sturdy trees in the woods, and make walking sticks as strong and as pretty as the one his great-great-granddaddy had made. He took good care of that filly, and she became a race horse that always won every race, but she was humble enough to pull a wagon at harvest time, too. And Jack took good care of his cow and her calf, and he soon had a fine herd of cows for himself. Jack made good money for himself and his family, and he truly became clever.

Now, I don't know if Jack was ever clever enough to finish that song, but I'm clever enough to know that I just finished this story.

STORY NOTES

In our family, slumgullion usually started out as a Sunday beef roast with gravy, and ended up as a pot of something filling but not as good as Sunday supper. The freshly made, more upscale version for our family was a combination of ground beef, noodles, onions, and tomato sauce that we called "goulash", although there was nothing Hungarian about it. In Columbus, Ohio, this dish became a casserole topped with cheese, known as "Johnny Marzetti"; originating in the 1920s, it is said to be named for the brother of the owner of Marzetti Restaurant.

For those uninitiated in the mealtime schedule of the Appalachian hills as well as the Southern U.S.: some older folks would tell you that supper is what we now call "lunch", and was usually the largest meal of the day, unless the preacher was coming over for Sunday dinner after his visits to congregation members. Dinner was usually a lighter meal, or second helpings from supper, but when the preacher was coming to eat —and he always paid a visit to the best cooks' homes, sometimes even brought his wife!—it was Thanksgiving and Christmas set on the best white tablecloth, never a slumgully meal!

The last line in the story is written the way my daddy said it. And the rest of the story is pretty much his words as best I can remember them. He would sing the song all the way through the story. I usually do, too, which makes an audience laugh, sing along, or groan.
This is one of the many tales about Jack. European in their origins, they are also tales of Juan, John, Hans, Ivan, and others. The character of the clever fool is an ages-old one, strongly rooted in Scots-Irish-Welsh heritage and well-known throughout the Appalachian region. But among the Affrilachian folktales, Jack, or his counterpart Janie, is

distinctly unique to the tales of the fool, not the trickster. Fool Jack, or silly Janie, survives foolishness, and usually gains something—wisdom, wealth, good fortune, a good life-partner—in spite of a serious lack of knowledge and common sense. Although he is called "clever" in the title of this story, he is rewarded in spite of a distinct lack of intelligent behavior.

On the other hand, the trickster is wise, knowledgeable, truly clever, and often scheming in order to succeed. He is John or Old John, and often John the Conqueror, a trickster-hero of mental distinction, inner strength and physical prowess who just happens to have the same first and proper name as "Jack"—I didn't know that Jack was a nickname for John until John F. Kennedy became the president of the United States. I guess he was clever, too.

You'll meet truly-clever John in a short time. But, first, I'd like to introduce you to Josephus.

Josephus

Josephus was born into servitude, enslaved from the day he was born. When he was about ten years old—his birth unrecorded, he had no idea exactly how old he was—Josephus was sold to a man who ran a ferry at an Ohio River crossing.

The ferryman told him what to do: "You help folks get on the ferry. You put their bags on the ferry. You help them off on the other side, and you put their bags off on the other side. You do what I tell you to do, 'cause you're too stupid to know how to do anything else."

Josephus, just a boy, didn't argue with the ferry man. He just lowered his eyes, and put his head down.

About five years passed. Now Josephus was a teenaged boy, big for his age—whatever it was—and strong. One day he said to the ferryman, "Sir, I know how to make the ferry go. I know how to pull it across the river by the rope, and I know how to pole it across when the water is muddy and low. If you want, you could take yourself a rest. I can make the ferry cross this river all by myself."

But the ferryman said no. "You just do what I tell you to do. You're too stupid to know how to do anything else."

Josephus got angry, and clenched his fists. But he lowered his eyes, and put his head down.

Five more years passed. Josephus was a man. He was tall, and strong, and he worked hard every day the ferry ran. One day he said to the ferryman, "Sir, I know you gettin' old now. And you need your rest. Why don't you just take a nap under that big maple tree? I can make the ferry go all by myself."

But the ferryman said what he'd said before, "No. You just help folks get on the ferry. You put their bags on the ferry. You help them off on the other side. You put their bags off on the other side. Stop askin' me to let you run the ferry, and just do what I tell you to do. You're too stupid to know how to do anything else!"

Then Josephus, now a man who could knock that ferryman down with one blow, took a deep breath. He lowered his eyes, and he put his head down.

Time passed, as it does, and a man from Marietta, Ohio came across the water, at some safe point along the Ohio River. Secretly, he was an abolitionist, working for the Underground Railroad, and he'd come to help Josephus gain his freedom.

He came to the ferry secured on the Kentucky side of the waters, and saw Josephus guarding the ferry. The old ferryman was asleep in the shade under that big maple tree.

The abolitionist boarded the ferry with Josephus' help and sat, as if awaiting the ride to Ohio, but he whispered, "Josephus, why do you stay here now? That man is asleep, and you could take the ferry to the other side *right now,* and escape. I could help you if you need. I wonder, why have you stayed here all this time, why do you stand here now, when if you just take the ferry, you could be free?"

Josephus said, "Sir, I can't. You see, I'm too stupid to know what to do. At least, that's what that man keeps telling me." Josephus nodded toward the sleeping ferryman.

"But at night," he continued with the hint of a grin, "when it gets dark, I must get a little smarter, 'cause I been helpin' folks run away across this part of the river for the past twenty years. And that man ain't caught me yet.

"He can call me what he wants to call me. I know who I am. And one day, when the time is right, I will take the ferry across this river myself, and be free."

My daddy told me this story, and he would end with the words, "You've got to know who you are. You've got to remember that an adjective—like "stupid"—is not your name.

"And you need to know these little stories, to know who you are."

STORY NOTES

This is a story that still puts a lump in my throat as I tell it. I have never cried during the telling, but the tears aren't far from the corners of my eyes. For this is the first story I remember my father telling about an escaping captive. It was told to help me escape my own petty but trying situations in school.

I was the only child of any culture but European-American in what was then known as "the fast learners," that skilled level of learning that is now designated as "gifted." My first-grade teacher hadn't believed I belonged in that class, but my second-grade teacher seemed to care if other children teased me, and showed respect for the skills of all her students. She left to get married, and returned as my third-grade teacher. But she wasn't always around to be a mentor and protector, and there were nights when I cried myself to sleep.

After dark, Daddy would come home from his second job. Everyone else would already be asleep. He would hear me tossing and turning, and invite me to come downstairs. There, we would share a midnight meal, leftovers and a glass of milk. While we ate, keeping our voices low enough to avoid awakening my mother, he would tell me stories like this one of Josephus. These midnight storytelling sessions didn't happen often, but I now realize what a gift they were. Remembering them has gotten me through much more than a bad day at school.

When I became a member of the Greater Columbus Arts Council's Artists-in-Schools program, I wanted to create a program in which I would share stories of the Underground Railroad. I didn't want to repeat the well-known stories that most Ohio students heard about African American heroes of the 19th century's freedom movement. The stories of Frederick Douglass, Sojourner Truth, Harriet Tubman, John Parker are important to our understanding of history and the present day, but a young woman in a juvenile detention center made it clear that they are shared often—and by many presenters. When she walked into the facility's library where I was ready to tell, her first words were, "Just don't sing 'Swing Low, Sweet Chariot'. Everybody that comes here for Black History Month sings 'Swing Low, Sweet Chariot'. And don't tell us anymore about Frederick Douglass and Harriet Tubman. Ain't there anybody else?"

So I told Dad's story of Josephus and a couple other tales that those young women had never heard. And I crossed "Swing Low, Sweet Chariot" off my list for the presentation.

From then on, I wanted to tell more of the lesser-known tales, and I started researching the three or four I could remember from those midnight meals, and a few tales told on travels down long roads or into unknown woods.

I wanted to tell more of the story of Josephus. But I couldn't find a historical source for it, and I thought that my father might have made it up. I would have to share it as a legend, rather than a work based in non-fiction, but I was determined to keep the story alive. Then I came upon the work of Mr. Henry Robert Burke.

The late Mr. Burke was a historian and folklorist in Marietta, Ohio; he was an extraordinary resource for information about the history of Southeast Ohio. The author of several books, he was the recipient of numerous awards for his research on the Underground Railroad. While working in Belpre, Ohio, I came across some of his writing in the local library, and discovered his very personal Underground Railroad Museum. When I returned home, I did an Internet search—no Google in those days, so it wasn't as easy as finding information can be today—for Mr. Burke's website, and found a link to a story. My heart just about stopped; I know I started to cry. For there was a name that I knew: Josephus.

According to Mr. Burke's research, Josephus was a code name for a slave who helped folks escape across the Ohio River for nearly fifty years, until the Emancipation Proclamation of 1863. At that time, those captives held in states that were in rebellion against the government during the American Civil War were declared to be free. Josephus worked from the

Virginia—now West Virginia—side of the Ohio River, near the mouth of Duck Creek. The trails of that area are now Ohio State Route 77, which crosses a bridge from Ohio into West Virginia.

Mr. Burke also stated that, in the 1800s, that part of the river was lower than it is today. It was possible to cross to freedom by "wading in the water" at some points along the Ohio River.

If I'd known Mr. Burke well enough, I would have hugged him! Instead, I prepared my daddy's story of Josephus, with a historical aside, crediting Mr. Henry Burke.

Four Tales of John

One · The Baby

John stole a suckling pig to cook for the hungry folks in the slave quarters. He cooked it slowly over a fire built in his little fireplace, in a drafty cabin where the wind shook the walls and made the firelight dance.

He'd asked the foreman for more food for the children, at least an extra supply of corn meal and some *fatback* to add flavor to the pot of greens or beans, or whatever the meager portion was for each household. When the foreman told John that the plantation owner wouldn't go for that, John stole that pig.

John kept the pot lid sealed as tightly as he good, so that the aroma of his cooking wouldn't draw attention. When the pig was tender and cooked through, John divided it up amongst the families and told them to keep their ears open for the sound of the foreman's footsteps, their hearts open to the possibility of escape, and their mouths shut, except for opening them to eat that pig.

Well, there'd been so many piglets born that season that the foreman and the plantation owner didn't notice one was missing. So, a few days later, John stole another one. He cooked it up, fed folks, and they kept their mouths shut, except for eating that pig.

When the third suckling pig disappeared, the foreman noticed. He told the plantation owner, who sent him to the slave quarters to see if he could learn anything about what was surely a theft.

The foreman walked softly, hoping to hear somebody talking about that missing pig. What he heard was a squeal, then another squeal. The noises came from John's cabin.

Well, it wasn't really John's cabin. He couldn't own anything except what he kept hidden in his head and heart. The foreman walked right in John's door, and looked around.

On the hearth, close to the blazing fire, was a basket. Something wiggled and squirmed under a blanket in that basket.

The foreman glared at John. "What's in that basket?" he asked.

"In the basket?" John repeated. "Oh, that's the baby."

"Baby?!?" The foreman was aghast. "John, you ain't got no family. Where'd you get a baby?"

"Well, sir," John said, "That baby's mama and daddy are real tired, and I told them I'd mind the baby tonight, so's they can get a good night's sleep."

The foreman walked a little closer to the basket. He tapped it with his foot. The thing under the blanket squealed.

"John," said the foreman, "that don't sound like a baby."

"Baby's sick," John said, "been makin' that noise so much his folks couldn't get a bit of rest. I told you 'bout that."

The foreman crouched at the side of the basket, and pulled the blanket aside. He saw a bald head, slightly pointy ears, beady eyes, and a big flat nose.

"John," said the foreman, "that is the ugliest baby I have ever seen in my life."

John sighed, "Well, if you think he's ugly, you should see his mama and daddy!"

The foreman couldn't stop himself from laughing. Then he took the piglet back to its pen, and he told the plantation owner that the suckling pig had somehow gotten itself free and run off.

He didn't say anything about finding "the baby" with John. After such a good laugh, he just couldn't tell on John.

STORY NOTES

A similar tale appeared as "Baby in the Crib" in Richard M. Dorson's collection titled *American Negro Folktales*[1]. I remember sneaking the book out of the reference section of the public library in Sharon, Pennsylvania and into the pile of books I had pulled from the stacks for my homework topic, a study of *"Romeo and Juliet."* I discovered that nothing in Dorson's book came close to the energy within tales told by my dad, my grandfather, or the other storytellers in my family. Nonetheless, it was good to see the stories preserved in print.

That's why I am grateful for the publication of my own versions of family tales. But I ask you, no, I *tell* you, to read the tales aloud, even if you're by yourself.

Stories born in the oral tradition need to be spoken, and heard.

1.   Richard M. Dorson. *American Negro Folktales*. (Greenwich, CT: Fawcett Publications, 1967).

Four Tales of John
Two · Pig and Possum

It wasn't long before another pig disappeared. That riled the plantation owner to no end. He didn't trust the foreman to do his job anymore. It seemed like the foreman was looking the other way a lot, and getting a bit flabby around the middle to boot. So the plantation owner decided he'd go down to the slave quarters himself, and see what he could see. He figured he'd be able to find that pig.

Everything was quiet in the rough little cabins. Not a sound came from any one of them. In the twilight, he could sure folks weren't asleep. Eyes watched through cracks in the weathered boards and from beyond the windows. Folks prayed silently, hoping there would be no hint of what John was doing.

But the plantation owner thought he smelled something that smelled truly tasty. He followed that aroma directly to John's door.

See, John had to make sure that what he was cooking was tender and that it hadn't gotten singed in that cooking pot hanging in the fireplace. John had removed the lid to check that pig, right about the time the plantation owner was traipsing around the cabins. John's timing was bad. The consequences would be worse.

John was a good worker, so he wouldn't be hung. But he would surely be whipped. Maybe he would, lose a finger or two, maybe even a hand for stealing. The plantation owner and his foreman relied on John's mind more than his hands. John was the one who could foresee changes in the weather, and discern the best times for planting and harvesting. John knew more about how to work the soil than anybody else. Folks in the big house might think he could do just fine without a hand.

And now John's hands were setting the table with one plate, one fork, one knife. He'd set the pot lid back in place. Soon he'd call folks by singing for them:

Tell all the world, John,
Tell all the world,
I know the other world's not like this.
Tell all the world, John,
Tell all the world,
I know the other world's not like this.
When Jesus shook the manna tree ...
I know the other world's not like this ...
He shook it for you and he shook it for me ...
*I know the other world's not like this.**

Well, *this* wasn't a time for singing. John's door opened. The plantation owner stood in the doorframe. He stood there, glaring at John and breathing hard in anger. Then his eyes rolled back in his head and he couldn't help saying, "Aah." All that hard breathing had filled his lungs with the wonderful aroma of John's cooking.

"John," said the plantation owner. "I smell something cooking in that pot. What you got in there?"

John said, "Possum."

"Possum?!?" The plantation owner couldn't believe that John had the nerve to tell a lie like that. "I have never smelled a possum cookin' and smellin' like that!"

"Yes, sir," John spoke humbly. "But you ain't never smelled *my* cookin'. I know how to cook up some possum, make it smell like supper in Heaven!"

"Well, that's fine, John, that's fine. I'll just have a taste o' that possum you're cookin'."

The plantation owner sat down in John's only chair, at John's homemade table. He picked up John's plate and knife and handed them to John. "Go over to that pot and cut off a chunk o' that 'possum' for me, John," he said with a big, knowing grin on his face.

"Yes, sir," John said. He took the knife and walked behind that man to get to the cooking pot in the fireplace. But he stopped, and looked at the back of that man's neck. Then John looked at the knife, and back at that man, and he held his breath and slowly raised the knife.

But John knew that, if anything happened to the one who thought he owned everybody, somebody else in the slave quarters might suffer. John would be killed. While he didn't mind that, others would be beaten, maybe slaughtered for letting John take that knife to the plantation owner's throat. So John just sighed, and walked over to the cooking pot.

He removed the lid, and cut off a chunk of that meat.

John brought the plate of steaming and juicy fixings to the table and set it before that plantation owner. He handed the man the knife. The man filled his mouth, and started to chew.

His pleasure in that first bite showed all over his face. He smiled and chewed, and savored the flavor. Then he remembered what he was eating and who cooked it, and how it probably got to that cooking pot.

The man swallowed, and a deep frown replaced his grin. His eyes squinted, and his lips thinned as he slowly spoke, "So, this is 'possum', eh, John?"

John looked surprised as he leaned forward and peered closely at what was on the plate. Then he shook his head with amazement.

"When it when in the pot, it was possum," John said. "Now, if it come out pig, that's not my fault!"

The plantation owner tried not to grin, but it was hard not to show how much he loved that food. He smacked his lips and licked his fingers. He cleared his plate, and found it hard to resist the urge to lick it clean. Then he told John he'd be back the next time John made "possum."

After that, every now and then, the plantation owner himself brought suckling pigs down to John. Then he left, and returned when the aroma of John's "possum" filled his nose with wonder. He and John, and everybody else in the slave quarters, ate better than they had in a long time.

STORY NOTES

*"Tell All the World" is a spiritual of hope and promise. It is used as a code in this story, as were many spirituals in the times of the Underground Railroad.

Zora Neale Hurston's version of "Possum or Pig" was published in the long-defunct magazine, *Forum*, number 76, in September 1926. It is also a traditional African-American folktale known throughout the Southern and Appalachian states. I heard it told many times, usually as I rode somewhere with my father.

I've tasted possum. Possum stew, to be exact, with white potatoes and carrots and onions in a light brown gravy, served with homemade biscuits. The meat was fork-tender, and looked pretty decent, although both the meat and the stew gravy were not as distinctly brown as the chunky beef stew that I loved.

I asked what it was. I was told, "Taste it. You'll love it," by my mother. I asked again, "But, what is it?" My father said, "Lie-roach-ketch-meddlers." Translation: eat it, be glad you got it, and don't ask what it is or where it came from.

But I kept asking, and eating. It tasted pretty good. And eventually, when my plate was clean, I got the answer I demanded.

I didn't want that answer.

Pop-pops had gone hunting, and shot two possums. He skinned the things, cut off heads and paws, drained and deboned the meat after cleaning out the innards. He washed the things, and cut up the meat, and parboiled it slowly in water with garlic, onions, black pepper and a touch of beer, until it was fairly tender. Then he shared the meat with his daughter, my mother, who turned it into a stew.

Upon discovering what we were eating, my little brother laughed. My little sister cried. I thought, too late to do anything but digest, and stew in the juices of my anger. I stewed by climbing into the cherry tree in our backyard, and pouting. Nobody seemed to care.

But I never sought vengeance, or held a grudge. How could I? I'd cleaned my plate, and almost asked for seconds!

I haven't eaten possum since then. I also usually turn down any meat that swims in medium-brown gravy, unless I know what it was before it was put in a pot.

Four Tales of John
Three · The Handsomest Man in the World

John was getting older and older. Such is the path of life. He spent less time following the horse-drawn plow. He spent more time sitting on a tree stump in the middle of the field than he did turning soil. His hands ached. His knuckles hurt. His knees were always sore, and his eyes strained to see his own feet. John figured he was fortunate to have all his fingers, seeing how much firewood he had chopped over the years.

John decided he'd done enough on that plantation, enough of the necessary work, and enough of his secret work, too. His secret forays away from the fields had not cost him a finger or a hand in punishment. His night raids into the pig sties to get food for the families in the slave quarters had resulted in close calls, but not hanging, as he feared. His planning and preparing people to run away toward the North had not been traced back to him. John had always figured he was too old to run away himself; seemed like he was born old. But now, John felt it was time for him to go.

The plantation owner was already dead and gone. Nobody *moaned* or mourned or missed that boss man after he died. But his two sons inherited the property. They worked everybody just as their father had, from sunrise to sun-rest, with a little time under the sycamore trees at the sun-high part of the day, so they could eat a *piddlin'* portion of corn cake and catch enough rest to work until dark.

Yes, it was time to go, thought John. He pulled himself up from the stump, and headed for the wide wrap-around porch of the big house.

There sat one young plantation owner, who was surprised to see John heading for the house. No slave was permitted on the front porch, except to serve cool beverages and deliver fans in the heat. John stopped at the steps, and kept his head down.

The young plantation owner shouted, "What you doin' here, John?"

"Comin' to ask you for my freedom, sir," John said quietly. With his eyes turned toward the ground, he continued, "I been workin' with the young folks, teachin' 'em what to do an' how to do it. I told 'em about checkin' the wind and the weather, about watchin' the trees and the critters for signs of what's comin' every season, and when and what to plant and how to feed it so it grows up strong and good to eat.

"And I think it's time for you to let me be my own free man, sir. You don't need me no more."

No person had ever been freed on that land. Some had disappeared. Many had died. But none had been set free. The young plantation owner said, "I've never heard such a thing, John. You askin' for your freedom? Why, you almost make me laugh, and I don't laugh easily, John. I haven't laughed in a very long time."

That statement gave John an idea.

"Well, sir, what if I make you laugh, laugh like you ain't laughed in the longest while? We could make it a bet. If I make you laugh, you set me free. If I don't, I stay here until I die."

The young plantation owner thought this was a fool's bet, one that John couldn't possibly win. He stood, hands on hips, and shouted for anyone within earshot to hear, "Yes, John, if you can make me laugh, I'll set you free. You got three chances to do it. I'll be lookin' for you once each mornin' for three days to try and make me laugh, hear?"

John nodded, "Yes, sir." Saying "sir" to a young man just a few years from boyhood, one who had never earned such respect, did not sit well with John. His stomach churned, but his mind started working on how to make that man laugh.

The prayers in the slave quarters that night were all for John. Everyone knew what he was trying to do. Even the plantation's overseer, the one people called "the foreman," had heard his employer make a bet with John. Folks gathered together in secret, and whispered prayers, "Please, let John get his freedom. Help John make that boy laugh."

At sunrise, under an orange and heated sky, John sat on his stump and oversaw the work in the fields. It was early, but folks from the slave quarters were always up and working at that time of day. They were shocked to see the plantation owner coming their way. They knew he was looking for John.

He didn't even make John stand to speak to him. He tipped his wide-brimmed hat and greeted the old man, "'Mornin', John."

"Oh, is that you, sir?" John shaded his eyes with his hand and looked directly at the plantation owner, something he was not wont to do. "Sun's so bright, it was hard to see you. But you know, now that I do, I have to tell you somethin'. Sir, you are a downright handsome man!"

The plantation owner was taken aback. He didn't know what to say. Figuring that this was some trick, he frowned as seriously as he could, and said, "That didn't make me laugh, John. And I've got things to do. But I'll be back tomorrow morning to see if you can make me laugh. You only got two chances left."

The day passed, a hard day, and a hot, humid night. The next morning, folks worked silently in the cotton fields. Folks did the cutting and the re-planting. Some did yard work. Other folks did the clothes-washing and the soap-making. A few were busy at fence-mending. Others tended the cattle, the horses, the chickens and the pigs. Several women bathed the children from the big house. They did whatever else needed to be done, but they didn't talk.

All over the land, folks listened for footsteps, for questions and replies. Every now and then, they glanced toward the big house, and then at John, who sat patiently on his tree stump. John only had two chances left, and this was the morning for his second attempt at freedom.

The sun was just above the tallest tree when folks saw the young plantation owner walking toward John. He stopped, and greeted John again, "'Mornin', John."

John shielded his eyes against the sunlight again, and said, with a sad look drawing his face toward his shirt collar, "'Mornin', sir. I got to tell you somethin'."

The plantation owner straightened up to his full height, for this sounded like the beginning of a confession. "You say you got somethin' to tell me, John?" he asked.

"Yes, sir, I do," said John. He looked toward his feet. "Yesterday, I told you a lie. I said you were downright handsome. That ain't true."

Folks stopped digging and moving. They stopped breathing. They couldn't believe that John had said something like that!

"That ain't true, John?" The plantation owner asked.

"No, sir, it ain't," John shook his head as he spoke. "You ain't downright handsome. Why, you the handsomest man I've ever seen in my life! I ain't ever seen a man look as good as you!"

The plantation owner caught himself starting to smile, but he forced that smile away, and said, "That ain't funny, John. I ain't sure why you said it, but that ain't gonna make me laugh today. You got one more chance for your freedom." His eyes scanned the people who were now trying not to look in his direction, and he walked away.

For the rest of the day, John sat on his stump, watching over the work better and with more kindness than any other overseer had.

The third morning was like the other two, hot and sweaty, just the beginning of the day's tribulations. But the people worked, and waited, and watched old John on that tree stump as he watched over them. They didn't have to wait very long for that young man to come looking for John.

He strode across the fields, his pace as hot as the early

sunlight, his eyes fixed on John. He stopped just a foot or so away from the old man. He didn't say good morning.

"John, I'm getting' tired of this gamble," he said, and his words felt hot against John's face. "What you gonna do today to try and make me laugh?"

"Well, sir," John said calmly. "I have to tell you somethin' first. Yesterday, I told you another lie. I said you was the handsomest man I'd ever seen. I been thinkin' about that, and that's not quite true.

"It's not?" The plantation owner didn't know what to expect.

"No, no, sir, it's not," John went on. You not the handsomest man *I've* ever seen. You the handsomest man *anybody* has ever seen. You are the handsomest man in the world!

"Why, you outshine the risin' sun. You make a good day look bad. You just such a good-lookin' man, you are *glorious* to behold!"

The plantation owner smirked, "I wish I could say the same thing about you, John."

John leaned back on his stump, and grinned. "Well, you could say it, sir, if you was as big a liar as I am!"

Even the birds stopped twittering to hear what might happen next. First, there was a choking sound, then some chuckles, then a full-blown, belly-shaking guffaw. The plantation owner couldn't stop himself from laughing, until he realized what he'd done, witnessed by everyone within shouting distance.

Folks all about were shouting and dancing with joy. Even the foreman, a stern man who's job was to oversee the work and discourage foolishness, was laughing as if he'd been in on the joke the whole time. And he had John's *manumission papers* in his pocket, ready for the young plantation owner to sign. The foreman knew folks, and he knew it was time for John to go.

John wasn't laughing. He was crying tears of relief and happiness. Someday he might laugh about it. But on that day, John had finally gained his freedom, and that was no laughing matter.

STORY NOTES

When I was a child and we visited elders, there was a distinction between cornbread and corn cake. Cornbread was made with buttermilk and no sugar; corn cake was a suppertime or dinnertime treat, made for rarely-seen and deeply-loved and respected relatives' visits, or when the preacher came to great-grandma's house for Sunday dinner. To my knowledge, Great-Aunt Kat, our relative and neighbor, never used sugar. I didn't particularly like her cornbread. It tasted sour to me, and I didn't know that was the flavor of real buttermilk. Aunt Kat and Uncle Stafford, and my Dad and Ma, would eat this baked or fried corn bread served with a big glass of buttermilk. Sour meal-bread plus sour milk equaled "No, thank you very much" from me.

Daddy also loved to put a piece of cornbread in a bowl with *clabbered* milk poured over it. This was called kushkush or couscous by some folks. Daddy's other "cush" recipe was leftover cornbread, mixed with onions and bacon or ham, served or eaten warm from the skillet. The names for this mixture can be traced to Africa's Arabic-language-speaking families, and the recipes for fried meal cakes and various types of mush, each unique to a specific culture or region and its available grains.

Dad said this was "real eatin", no matter what it was called.

Dad told a handful of tales in which John got his freedom through trickery or riddles. I only remember a couple of them, the one I've written here, and one that most folks know as "The Freedom Riddle," in which John unwittingly gives the correct response to a riddle that was meant to keep him enslaved. In other "freedom riddle" tales, John posed a question to his "marster," and gained freedom because his riddle was too difficult to be solved. In some of these stories, the riddle was a rhyme or song. I truly wish that Dad had recorded them all.

A version of this story appeared as "A Riddle for Freedom" in William J. Faulkner's *The Days When Animals Talked: Black American Folktales and How They Came to Be*[1]. Angela Shelf Medearis used Faulkner's story, which is said to be based upon a true incident, as the basis for her picture-book, *The Freedom Riddle*[2]. A similar story appeared in Virginia Hamilton's *The People Could Fly: American Black Folktales*, as "The Riddle Tale of Freedom."

1. William J. Faulkner. *The Days When Animals Talked: Black American Folktales and How They Came to Be.* (Trenton, NJ: Africa World Press, Inc., 1993).

2. Angela Shelf Medearis. *The Freedom Riddle.* (New York: Lodestar Books, 1995).

3. Virginia Hamilton. *The People Could Fly: American Black Folktales* (New York: Alfred A. Knopf, 1985).

Four Tales of John
Old John and Death

Old John had lived a long time, much longer than even he had expected. He'd seen freedom taken by some and given to others, including himself. But freedom didn't stop John from having to work to put food on the table, or firewood on the stack. And that's what John was doing this day, toting firewood back to his cabin.

The homebound path was crooked and uneven, and the day burned against John's leathered skin. His aches and pains seemed as heavy as that firewood. He was tired of this journey, and tired of his life. John threw the bundle of wood to the ground, and fell on his knees.

He cried out, "Death, oh, Death, I wish you'd deliver me from my burdens!"

To John's surprise, up jumped Death.

Death stared at John with eyes as deep as the grave, and held out a hand as cold as the iciest winter night. Then Death spoke, and his words chilled the air, "You have called me here, old man. Shall I now relieve you of the burdens of your life?"

John swallowed hard. "Uh, no," he said, "I wasn't callin' you for that. I was callin' you to help me carry this firewood home. But I've changed my mind. I think I'll jus' handle it myself."

John stood quickly, picked up the firewood, and walked home with the spryness and speed of a much younger man.

✺ ✺

STORY NOTES

Aesop is said to have declared that, if every wish was granted, we could know the sorrow of it. My mother said, "Be careful what you wish for. You might get it." My father told this version of an Aesopic fable, and said, "Death comes like a friend, if you live right. But don't call him if you're not ready to meet him."

Smart people, yes?

The legendary John of Affrilachian folklore was a descendant of the smartest of men and women. They had been taken captive in Africa, brought to the Americas against their will, and disenfranchised. Gone were their opportunities to openly use their ancestors' languages and practice their religions. Gone were the old-wisdom systems in which they might be educated, and the right to call themselves by their families' ancestral names. But they knew that no one can take what you carry in your head and heart. That knowledge, that hope and strength, were instilled in their children, and their children's children. That lesson, through stories, was offered to me.

Such oppression could not last. Like warriors of the Motherland, some folks fought for freedom from forced labor and abuse in the cotton fields, the tobacco fields, the sugar-cane fields, the stables, the orchards, and the plantation "big house." Folks fought with the strength of their bodies and the courage and convictions of their hearts. Others just up and ran away, making the dangerous journey to the "Promised Land" of hope and freedom on secret trails that eventually became the Underground Railroad.

Some folk engaged in a battle of wits that helped others to escape, while they remained on the plantations and in the fields as clandestine warriors and covert intelligence agents. Their stories became legends and humorous tales, some about a man named John.

The Devil and the Farmer's Wife

An old man lived on a hill. He had a wife, a son, a cow, and a farm on hardscrabble land, and he wasn't sure if any one of these was worse trouble than the other three.

One sticky-hot summer morning, with no breakfast in his belly, his back aching, and his knee bones snapping and cracking, that old man hitched his cow to the plow, and started his work. His wife wasn't speaking to him, and his ornery son was still asleep. On top of everything else, that cow refused to pull. She just plopped herself down and wouldn't get up.

The old man threw up his arms and shouted to the sky, "I have been *cursed*!" And, "I wish that ol' Devil would come and take one of his curses back!"

Up jumped the Devil. He was short and sturdy, as mean-looking as a boar. He pointed at the old man with a long, coal-filthy fingernail, and he said, "Heard ya. And I've come to take one of your troubles away. I think I'll take this cow."

"Oh, not my cow!" cried the old man. "I can't get the plowin' done without her!"

"Well then, I'll take your son," said the Devil.

"Oh, not my son!" cried the farmer. "I'm getting' old. I'll never get the work done around here without him!"

"Then I'll take your wife," said the Devil.

"Oh, not my ... well ... ," said the old man, and he thought a bit. "Well, you can have *her* with my blessin'. And I hope the two of you will be very happy."

The Devil looked around for that old woman. She was snapping string beans into a big cast iron pot. The mean on her face was a match for the Devil's. She looked up and saw him standing before her, which didn't scare her a bit. It just made her angry. She stood up, ready to cuss. Before she could say a word, the Devil picked her up and threw her over his shoulder like a sack of potatoes. And off he trotted toward the crossroads.

By the time he got there, the devil thought his back would break. "Old woman," he gasped, "you are one hell of a load!"

Well, whilst dangling off the Devil's back, she kicked him with the toe of one of her work boots, got him right in the back-ribs. Down they both went, tumbling through the trap door at the crossroads, down and down to the gates of Hell.

All the while, the Devil held onto that woman for dear life. He didn't dare let go of her, for fear she'd beat the tar out of him as they fell.

When they landed on hard ground before the gates, it turned out the dang things were locked. The Devil finally set that woman down so he could find the key. Before he could draw the key to Hell from his pocket, that woman had kicked down the gates! The old woman stomped into Hell and hollered, "Where's the kitchen? I'm hungry! I'm ready to eat!"

A little demon came running to see what all the commotion was. The Devil told him to bring chains for that old woman. That little demon came back with the chains and another little demon, who was supposed to help get that woman locked into them.

Didn't happen.

That old woman kicked them both with the toe of her work boot, nearly knocking their little brains out of their skulls. They scurried away, dizzy as a whirlwind, squealing like pigs.

So the Devil summoned two more little demons. He told them to grab the woman, put her in a sack, and throw her into the fiery furnace. Well, she kicked them both with the toe of her boot, nearly breaking their backs in two. They crawled off, sore and mewling like calves.

Then the old woman stomped around, looking for the kitchen. She screeched and cussed and kicked at everybody and everything. Big demons, little demons, and imps of the smallest size went scurrying in every direction, looking for hiding places.

The Devil was so scared that he stayed outside the broken-down gates. Nine little demons popped their heads up over the wall, and begged, "Please, Daddy, take her back to wherever you found her! She's gonna kill us all!"

Well, it took him a while to corral that woman. But the Devil managed to throw her back over his shoulder, and he started running up and out of his trap door, and back toward the old man's farm on the hill.

The old man could hear his wife screeching and fussing as she and the Devil approached the house. Before the old man could latch on the door, the Devil rushed in and threw that old woman on the floor. She got up and kicked the Devil him in the shins. Then she went back to her string beans.

"Old man, I've returned your old woman to you," said the Devil as he rubbed his shins. "I have to tell you, I never knew what Hell was until I met your wife. I don't know how you put up with her! But I've brought her back."

Old man said, "Devil, what will you give me for keepin' her? If you don't give me somethin' that makes my life a bit more worthwhile, I'm not gonna take her back. I'm gonna send that woman back to Hell with you, and you can keep her there."

You know the Devil didn't want that. He told the old man that he would promise anything, and he would keep his promise as long as that old man kept that hellacious old woman.

"Then promise me that you won't bother me or my kinfolk or my cow or my farm ever again," said the old man.

The Devil agreed, and he kept his promise. To him, it seemed like the better part of the deal.

After that, things changed on the hill. The soil turned rich, and the old man's crops grew in abundance. The cow pulled the plow as if she were still a young heifer. The old man's son grew in wisdom, and he started helping with the farm work early instead of sleeping in. The farm prospered. And the old woman mellowed like a fine wine, for the old man treated her with an ever-growing love and a deepening respect.

He realized that only a woman like his wife could go to Hell, beat the Devil, and come back again.

✥ ✥

There once was a farmer who lived on a hill;
If he ain't dead, he's livin' there still.

Well, the devil came down to the man at the plow;
Said, "I've come to take one o' your kin now".

With a right leg, left leg, east west, half-a-leg,
Jump back, Devil, don't you come no more.

Well, the man cried, "Please don't take my son;
There's work on the farm that's gotta be done."

"You can take my wife, and with all of my heart,
I hope the two of you never need part."

With a right leg, left leg, east west, half-a-leg,
Jump back, Devil, don't you come no more.

Old Devil he hoisted her onto his back
And he toted her off like an ol' gunnysack.

He carried her down to the fork in the road,
Devil said, "Old woman, you're a hell of a load."

With a right leg, left leg, east west, half-a-leg,
Jump back, Devil, don't you come no more.

Down they went to the gates of Hell;
Devil said, "Old woman, I'll scorch you well."

But the gates were closed and before he knocked,
She upped with her boot and kicked off the lock.

With a right leg, left leg, east west, half-a-leg,
Jump back, Devil, don't you come no more.

Up stepped a little demon with a handful of chains.
She upped with her boot and knocked out his brains.

Up stepped a little demon to put her in a sack
She upped with her boot and broke his back.

With a right leg, left leg, east west, half-a-leg,
Jump back, Devil, don't you come no more.

Then nine little demons peeped over the wall,
Said, "Take her back, Daddy, or she'll kill us all!"

Devil said, "What to do I cannot tell;
You ain't fit for Heaven, and you're tearin' up Hell!"

With a right leg, left leg, east west, half-a-leg,
Jump back, Devil, don't you come no more.

So the Devil hoisted her onto his back
And toted her home like an ol' gunnysack.

He carried her over three fields and more
'Til he finally came to the old man's door.

With a right leg, left leg, east west, half-a-leg,
Jump back, Devil, don't you come no more.

Now the old man was peekin' through a crack,
When he seen the old devil a-bringin' her back.

Devil said, "Man, would you be so kind
As to take her back? I've changed my mind."

With a right leg, left leg, east west, half-a-leg,
Jump back, Devil, don't you come no more.

Man said, "What you give me for taking her in?"
Devil said, "No more than the wages of sin.

"I've been a Devil all my life,
But I never knew Hell 'til I met your wife!"

With a right leg, left leg, east west, half-a-leg,
Jump back, Devil, don't you come no more.

Man said, "If you want to be rid of this hen,
You'll never bedevil my family again."

That devil, he cried, that devil he howled,
But he never came back to the man at the plow.

With a right leg, left leg, east west, half-a-leg,
Jump back, Devil, don't you come no more.

This oughtta show what a woman can do.
She can take on a husband, and the devil, too.

And it proves that women can outdo men;
They can go through Hell and come back again.

With a right leg, left leg, east west, half-a-leg,
Jump back, Devil, don't you come no more.

With a right leg, left leg, east west, half-a-leg,
Jump back, Devil, don't you come no more.[1]

🙠 🙣

STORY NOTES

This story is, as best I can remember it, Dad's spoken-word version of an Appalachian ballad. Sometimes he'd sing it, sometimes he'd tell it. Spoken or sung, Daddy never shared it within my mother's earshot. I guess you can understand why.

If the Devil appeared in a story told by Dad, he didn't just walk into the scene. He jumped up, or popped up, or appeared with some kind of special effects or startling sound. Dad was good at startling sounds and vocal special effects.

Pop-pops, on the other hand, just said something like, "There was the Devil himself, dressed in a red silk suit ...." You'll read that story a little farther along, in the chapter, "Spookers & Haints."

There are many, many versions of this piece about the old woman and the Devil. I didn't know it was a ballad when I was a child. I don't know that my father ever referred to it as one. From research, I now know that it was collected by Francis James Child among *The English and Scottish Popular Ballads*, and is listed there as Child Ballad #278, "The Farmer's Curst Wife." Appalachian ballad lovers know it as "The Devil and the Farmer's Wife."

I have shared the verses that I remember of "The Devil and the Farmer's Wife" at the end of the story. The Chorus may be added after each verse, or between every two verses, but is traditionally sung twice at the end:

> *With a right leg, left leg, east west, half-a-leg,*
> *Jump back, Devil, don't you come no more.*

1. Francis James Child. *The English and Scottish Popular Ballads.* (Boston and New York, Houghton, Mifflin and Company, 1886 – 1898).

SPOOKERS AND HAINTS

I just couldn't resist including one more tale of John, even though, in the first story of this section, his character is wicked. The John that you'll meet in this section resides in the realm of haunts and hellish beings. A "Wicked John" tale seemed like the perfect connection to the last story in the "Folks" section, and a good segue to two spookier tales.

The other two stories are my favorites from the bedtime stories my father told—yes, bedtime stories. Daddy had a slightly twisted sense of what was appropriate to tell children in the dark at the end of the day. I loved it!

John and the Devil

Men and women both regretfully respected and feared John, for he hammered out meanness upon the backs and minds of others just as he hammered out the perfect iron horseshoes and wagon wheels he made in his blacksmith shop.

He was tall and well-sinewed, with strong features and a perfect smile, a smile that had fooled a poor woman into becoming his wife. That smile drew strangers into his smithy, too, where John would feed strangers a fine meal, for no one from his town would come for a visit. Even a mean man desires company from time to time.

One morning, a feeble old man came to the smithy, and leaned in the doorway until John invited him to sit in his own rocking chair and have something to eat. John had his wife fix a plate and a pitcher. He fed that old man a sumptuous meal, and went back to his hammer and forge.

As John worked, the old man set aside the food and drink, stood without a hitch, straightened himself to a great height, and changed into a robust, strong gentleman with white hair and a white beard. This changed man wore a white robe, and carried a huge golden key in one strong hand.

John knew that the once-feeble old man was not a man at all.

He introduced himself as St. Peter. "I was sent here to see if you was as mean as folks been tellin' us when they get to the Pearly Gates. They said your heart was as hard as coal, but it seems like you got a little soft spot somewhere in it.

"So I won't give a bad report when I get back to Heaven. And for the kindness you've shown me, I'll grant you three wishes. What do you want, John? What do you need?"

Well, John looked around the smithy, and his eyes settled on that rocking chair. "St. Peter," he said, "I get tired of folks just ploppin' down in my chair without bein' invited, when I need for it to be ready for me to sit down whenever I'm tired. So, I'd appreciate it if you made it hold a body's backside in place if somebody sits down without my invitin' them to do so. Keep 'em stuck in my rockin' chair, and rockin' like a boat, until I tell them they can stop."

St. Peter didn't like the wish, but he nodded once, and said, "Done."

"Now, how about doin' somethin' with my hammer, too?" John asked. "Folks just pick it up without askin,' and I don't like 'em touchin' it. Boys run in here and take it out to break rocks and such. How 'bout makin' it so, if a body so much as touches my hammer, that somebody can't stop hammerin' until I say they can stop?"

St. Peter shook his head at the thought, but he said, "Done."

"Last wish," said John, and he rubbed his chin as he did some heavy thinking. "I got a fine rose bush growin' by the door, blooms blood-red roses and always full of thorns. That don't stop folks from stealin' the blooms, or breakin' off switches for their horses and such. So, I want that thorn bush to grab onto anybody who touches it except me. Grab onto 'em, and hold 'em, and pull 'em down into the middle of it, and keep 'em there until I say they can get out."

John's last wish vexed St. Peter to no end. But, "Done," was all he said. And he was gone.

Weeks passed, and months. John irritated his poor wife in much the same way he had St. Peter, with cruel wishes and mean words, as heavy as his hammer and as hard as his anvil. Exasperated, his wife said, "The devil take you!"

And, as she went back into the house, a little devil no taller than your kneecap appeared at the smithy door.

"Hey, John," said the little devil, "Daddy sent me to fetch you. Come on, you got to go to Hell, a place worse than the hell you been sending your wife to every day."

John went on with his work. He took his time finishing an ax head, then he started working on another one. Tired of standing, the little devil sat himself down in John's rocking chair. By St. Peter's grace, that rocking chair started shaking itself back and forth like Noah's ark in that storm. The poor little devil got seasick, and he tried to get back out of that chair. But his backside was stuck to the seat as if he'd been glued into it, and his poor little head kept whacking the back of the chair. He begged John to help him get free.

"I'll get you outta that chair," John promised, "if you go on back to your daddy, and never bother me again."

The little devil agreed. John said, "Stop rockin'." The chair stopped rocking. And, in a puff of blue smoke, the little devil was gone.

Not even a whole day had passed before John had another row with his wife. She fussed at him, he yelled at her, she cried, and he laughed. She sniffled and snuffled, "The ... devil ... take you," and headed for the kitchen.

And another little devil, a bit bigger than the first one, appeared at the door of the smithy.

"John, my daddy said you gotta come with me. He told me not to let you get out of makin' the trip. You got away from my little brother, but you ain't gonna get away from me. Put down your work, and come on," said the little devil. He walked into the smithy and grabbed the hammer right out of John's hand.

By St. Peter's grace, that hammer started pounded at the anvil, the ground, the air, up and down, left and right, yanking that little devil around like a rag doll. He was getting dizzy, but he couldn't seem to let go of that hammer. He begged John to make the hammer stop.

"I'll make my hammer stop hammerin' if you promise to go away and never bother me again," said John.

That little devil agreed. John said, "Stop hammerin'." And the hammer dropped from the little devil's hands. He disappeared in a puff of green smoke.

Seemed like John got all full of himself after that. He yelled at his wife for nothing at all, and he dared her to sit in his chair or to touch his hammer. She didn't know why. All she knew was that she was through with John. "I am going back to my mother's house! And I hope and pray the devil comes for you!"

John smirked, "Let him come." He went back to his smithy and he waited on the Devil.

He wasn't there for more than a minute when he heard a voice at the door: "JOHN!"

There was the Devil himself, dressed in a red silk suit and red patent leather shoes. His horns were steaming and his eyes glowed like hot coals. He grinned, and held out his hand, "John," he said, "you may have troubled my boys, and made them promise to leave you be, but your old woman has tried to send you to me three times now. And this third time, you are goin' with me!"

John set his jaw, and yelled at the devil, "Don't talk to me as if I'm one of your sons. You can't make me do a thing, not even if you take a switch to me!"

"Why, I can and I will!" shouted the Devil. "I'll switch you as if you were my ridin' horse, John!"

The Devil snapped a thorny switch off John's rose bush. The bush reached out and yanked him right into the middle of it, and it held on with piercing thorns and curling vines. The Devil screamed like a baby girl. John laughed.

"You want outta my rose bush, you gotta promise that you won't bother me anymore, not you nor your kin. You gotta promise that you and our kin will leave me alone forever!"

"I promise!" shouted the Devil. John said, "Stop holdin'!" The thorns and vines let go. The Devil disappeared in a cloud of red smoke. And that was that.

Some folks say the good die young. Those same folks thought John was too mean to ever die.

They were wrong.

John found himself heading up the heavenly stairs to the Pearly Gates. St. Peter opened the gates up just a crack, saw John, and said, "No need of you knockin.' Been checking your account, and you have toted up a slew of wicked, so much that what little good you did for me doesn't even count.

"You can't get in here, John," said St. Peter. He shut the gates, and made sure they were locked.

So John headed back downstairs. When he arrived at his smithy, he continued down the other stairs, all the way to the gates of Hell. And who should be peeking through the gate but those two little devils. They screamed when they saw John. They hollered for their daddy. And the Devil himself came running to the gates, to help his sons set the latch and double-bar them, in case John had his hammer in hand.

"Don't come any closer!" shouted the Devil. You're not getting' in here! Go see St. Peter! He said you were nice to him once."

"Already seen St. Peter," said John. "Guess I wasn't nice enough. He wouldn't let me in there. And if you won't let me in here, well, I don't know where else to go!"

The devil pulled a piece of coal out of the fiery furnace and tossed it over the gate to John. "You mean enough, John," he said, "you are downright wicked! You take that piece of coal, and you make your own hell."

John took the coal, and he faded away. Some say he carries it still. In death, he has no place to go, so the wicked spirit of John still wanders the earth. You can tell when he's coming by the little spark of light he carries. You'll see the light, but you better hope you don't see John.

STORY NOTES

There are so many variants of this story and so many storytellers sharing them that I hesitate to tell it. The best known are probably versions adapted from Richard Chase's presentation in *Grandfather Tales[1]* It is credited to Mrs. Yowell and her daughter Alois, and to Peck Daniel. The story speaks of a fire-bush or quince instead of a rose bush. My dad said that the rose bush that grew against the lattice on our back porch was a cutting from John's thorny roses; Pop-pops agreed, adding that he had given the cutting to my mother when she and Dad bought the house. Both of them stuck to that story, and I believed it until I was grown. If you had ever fallen into those thorns and vines, you might have believed it, too.

Zora Neale Hurston's *Mules and Men[2]* includes the story, recounted by Mack Ford, of Big Sixteen—named for his shoe size—who was so mean he killed the devil and was given a coal by the devil's widow; that is the explanation for the "Jack O'Lantern" seen in the woods. Such variants of the tale attempt to explain the gaseous swamp or forest light known as the will-o-the-wisp, foxfire, or ghost light. John supposedly put that piece of hellfire in a gourd or pumpkin, to create a lantern he would forever carry on his search for a home after death.

The tale of John and the Devil is even commemorated on the Jack-O-Lantern Branch Heritage Trail at the Booker T. Washington National Monument in Hardy, Virginia.

Now, why is this story in my "Spookers & Haints" section, and not the story of the Devil and the farmer's wife? The Devil returns the old woman to her old man. At the end of her story, she is alive and well. Spookers are creatures of the shadows, but they're not necessarily or always dead. Haints are dead things, just one type of spooker, and usually far worse to encounter.

John is dead at the end of his story, and still wandering the earth. A haint, if ever there was one.

1. Richard Chase. *Grandfather Tales.* (Boston: Houghton, 1948).

2. Zora Neale Hurston. *Mules and Men.* (London: K. Paul, 1936).

Jack Finds His Fear

Young Jack came back from the war as a different young man than the one who had left to fight for the Union. He was still a bit dim-witted, and terribly lazy, but he wasn't afraid of anything anymore. Seemed like what he'd seen in the war had knocked the fear right out of him.

One morning, Jack's mama caught him standing on the roof of the barn, just tippy-toed on the very edge of that roof, and staring toward the rising sun.

Mama screamed, "Jack! What are you doin' up there???"

Jack calmly stated, "I'm tryin' t'catch the sunrise. Nothin' like feelin' the first rays of the sun on your face, Mama."

"Well, come down here and catch 'em on the ground, child!" Jack's mama fussed. And Jack came down and stood beside his mama. He wasn't a bit concerned about what he'd done.

That very evening, Jack's mama caught him with his fingertips in the fire, not yet touching the flames but terribly close.

Mama screamed again, "Jack! What are you doin'?"

"Dropped my tater in there, Mama," said Jack. "I was gonna pick it out. Don't worry. I'm quick. I won't get burnt."

But Mama yanked Jack away from the fireplace, and used a long fork to get the potato out of the fire. She handed Jack that fork, took his for her own baked potato, and shook her head.

"Child, ain't you afraid of anything?" she asked.

"No, ma'am, I ain't got any fears," Jack said with a smile.

"Why, Jack," said his mother, and she almost cried, "Anybody with half a grain of sense knows that sometimes you have to be afraid of somethin'. It's what keeps you cautious. It's what helps you stay safe.

"Honey, you got to find some fears if you're gonna survive in the world," she went on. But Jack ate his baked potato, blazing hot and right off the fork. Then he kissed his mama goodnight, and went to bed.

While Jack slept safely under a newly made quilt, Mama spent most of the night thinking. What could she do to help her son get that common-sense thing called "fear"?

By sunrise, Mama had a plan for Jack. She secured a half-loaf of freshly baked bread in a kerchief, then wrapped some cold bacon in a napkin, and put it all in a tote sack into which she stuck a few apples. Then she woke her son and sent him on his way.

"I'm sendin' you out to find your fear, Jack," she said. She wiped away a tear with the hem of her apron, but she spoke with a firmness that belied her own concerns.

"I don't want you to come back until you've found it, hear?"

Well, Jack didn't know where to look for fears. But he didn't want to disappoint his mama. So he said, "Yes, Ma'am," and he blew her a kiss, then down the road he went.

It was a long road, and it didn't lead to any fears. Jack knew where it went, from the farm to the town, passing by the woods and some other farms and households. Jack didn't see anything fearsome along the way. He saw a few scarecrows, and the crows who perched on their heads; he saw grumpy field hands and a bull who snorted at him. He saw filthy children who skipped along beside him and asked a thousand questions while they picked their noses. But he didn't see anything that resembled a fear.

At noon, Jack stepped off the road and into the woods. He

figured he might find some fears there. He saw a dead rabbit, and a few snakes, and a bear. But he didn't see any fears. He heard things he couldn't see, rustlings and buzzings and chirpings and growls. But they didn't sound like fears to Jack.

By evening, Jack was out of the other side of the woods, in a part of the country that he didn't know. Shadows grew longer before him as he walked away from the setting sun. He wondered how far away from his home and his mama he might be.

Jack was tired of looking for his fear.

That's when Jack came upon a big house, set high on a hill overlooking the countryside. Its door was gone, and the windows were broken. The shutters hung sadly in the window frames. The walls needed painting and the roof needed mending. The whole thing needed some tender loving care.

But on the crooked porch steps sat a man.

He looked as sad and needy as that house. So Jack walked up to him and sat down beside him.

"Good evenin', sir," said Jack. "Do you mind if I sit a spell with you and have a bite to eat? I'd be happy to share what my mama packed for me."

The man shook his head, no thank you. "But you can sit here a while," he said, "at least until the darkness comes."

Jack thanked the man, and opened up his tote sack. But he noticed the man was looking him up and down. So Jack looked back.

"You ain't from around here," the man said to Jack. "I know everybody around here."

"No, I'm not from here, "Jack said. "I'm from yonder, and a bit farther than that. Came home from the war just a few days ago"

Jack pulled an apple from his sack. The man kept staring at him. "What you doin' here, then?" asked the man.

"Lookin' for my fear. Mama says I need to find it, but I'm not sure where to look. Mister, do you know where I might find some fears?" Jack smiled a big friendly smile as he spoke to the man.

"Fear? Why, if you stay here tonight, you'll find some fears, I guarantee you that," said the man. He looked toward the setting sun as he spoke, then he looked at his pocket watch.

"This place is cursed and haunted," he continued. "It's been in my family for near a hundred years, but ain't nobody lived here since, well ... ain't nobody lived here for quite some time.

"If you want to find your fears, this is the place to look. You won't last the night, probably run home to yer mama 'round midnight. But if you do stay, if you're still here in the mornin', then the house is yours for a cheaper than fair price, and you're welcome to it. It'll be good to have a young soldier for my neighbor. You're welcome to farm the land. Simply give me a portion of your take each year, if there's a profit. You're welcome to come down to my property and call on me and my daughter, too.

"That is, if you're still here come morning.'"

The man stood, and headed for a smaller, well-kept farm house in the valley. He nodded at Jack. He said, "I hope to see you tomorrow, but I doubt that I will."

Well, there was Jack, alone on the porch of a doorless haunted house. He hadn't eaten his apple yet, hadn't taken a bite out of it. He thought about apples roasted in the fireplace; the thought took him into the house.

Sure enough, there was a fine fireplace, and dry firewood that somebody had left beside it. Jack had his matches and he had his apples. And he didn't mind sleeping on the hearth. So Jack started a fire, and emptied his tote sack. He sat on the hearthstones and prepared to toss an apple into the fire.

"Ooooooh, watch out!" somebody shouted down the chimney. "I'm fallin'!" And down the chimney, with a thump and a bump and thump and a crash into the fire, fell two big, bare feet.

Jack looked at the feet. Then he looked at the apple in his hand. "Well, it's a good thing you warned me," Jack said. "I was about to put my apple in the fire. You woulda smashed it!"

Jack set the apple on his mama's kerchief, and pulled the feet out of the fire. They smoked a bit, and smelled a bit, but they were in pretty good shape. Jack whacked them together like a pair of dusty shoes, set them on the hearth, and grabbed a piece of bacon.

Before he could bite off a bit, he heard something else high up in the chimney. "Ohhhhh, watch out!" somebody shouted. "I'm fallin'!"

Before Jack could say "I thought you already fell," down the chimney came two big legs in a pair of mildewed pants that landed in the fire.

"Well," said Jack, "You must go with these feet." He took the legs out of the fire, shook them out and straightened the pants legs. Then he set them near the feet.

He bit into that bacon and tried to chew it up before anything else would happen. If there's feet and legs fallin' down the chimney, he thought, there's probably more to come.

And there was. "Owwwww, watch out!" somebody shouted. "I'm fallin'!" Jack swallowed his bacon. Thump, bump, thump, crash! There was a torso, arms attached, hands sticking out of a raggedy shirt that caught fire as the whole thing fell into the fireplace.

"Now, look," fussed Jack, "It would've been quicker if you'd fallen down in one piece. And your about to burn yourself up!" Grabbing one hand, Jack yanked the torso out of the flames. He stomped on the arms and beat the chest to stop the shirt from burning. With every blow, he heard a voice somewhere up in the chimney: "Ouch! Ooch! Ouch! Oh! Ow!"

When the shirt had stopped burning, Jack grabbed the torso and tossed it down beside the legs and feet. Then he stood, and waited, anticipating ...

"Eeeeee, watch out! I'm fallin'!"

And bammity, bammity, BAM, there in the fire was a big old head, the eyes staring at Jack, the mouth hanging open and moaning, "Ohhhh. ..."

Jack snatched the head up by its hair, walloped it against the hearth to put out the fire burning its nose, and threw it down next to the feet.

"There!" Jack cried in exasperation. "That should be all of you. Now, pull yourself together!"

Slowly, the feet attached to the legs, the legs slid against the torso, and the head rolled itself into place on the neck. With a slurpy sound, the whole thing sucked itself together. Then it stood in front of Jack.

It grinned at Jack for a second, and disappeared.

"Well, that was an experience," said Jack. He sat down to finish his bacon and bread. Then, into the fire he tossed an apple, quickly rolling it around with a thin piece of firewood instead of with his hands, which would have pleased his mama.

When the skin was soft and the insides were squishy, Jack rolled the apple out of the fireplace and onto the hearth to cool. That's when the plinking and clinking started at the top of the stairs.

Jack stepped into the hallway and looked up at the landing. There were bones, big ones and small ones, rolling down the steps toward him. They pulled themselves into a skeleton. A skull bounced down the stairs after them, and landed at Jack's feet.

"Are you afraid?" asked the skull.

"Not really," said Jack. "I'm bored. Wanna play a game?"

Jack looked around for something they could use to play. Then he looked back at that skull and those bones. Jack got an idea.

"When I was soldierin', we played a game called tenpins. We used a wooden ball and ten pins for it. Now, we don't have any pins, but if I break you back down into pieces and parts, and I rip off your skull..."

Jack set up his pins, arm bones and leg bones and parts of the spine, whatever stood straight and tall. Jack grabbed his ball, the chattering skull of that skeleton he'd just torn apart. He wondered if it minded being dismantled again.

"Probably doesn't mind a bit," Jack said to himself as he set up the game. "He was in pieces and parts before we started conversin'."

With a swift swing of his arm, Jack rolled that skull. Clink and clunk and crash, all the pins fell down.

"Your turn!" Jack shouted. Then he realized there was nobody to take a turn, for his opponent was also his set of pins and ball.

"Sorry," said Jack. I guess you can't take a turn. I guess that means I win!"

There was no response. The fire crackled in its fireplace and the crickets chirped outside the doorless entryway, and that was all that Jack heard, until those bones clinked and rolled a bit, and disappeared.

Jack wondered what he'd do for the rest of the night. "Might as well go to sleep," he said. He turned toward the hearth, and there in front of his face was a hand.

That hand floated before his eyes, and glowed as if it were made of moonlight. It curled its finger for Jack to follow. Well, he didn't have anything else to do, so he followed. Then the hand pointed at a door, and slid right through it. Jack couldn't slide through a wooden door, so he opened it and found the hand floating over some stairs that led to a dank, dark cellar.

Down Jack went, led by the soft white glow of that hand. But the way was still dark, and Jack could hardly see. He stopped.

"If I try to make my way down these steps any farther, I might fall and break my neck. My mama would be pretty upset about that. I'm not followin' you anymore, unless you can give me a bit more light."

The hand snapped its third finger and thumb together. A spark shot out from that snap and lit the fingers like tapers in a candelabra. Their flames brightened the whole cellar.

"That's better," said Jack. He followed the hand down the stairs and into a corner, where old boards and broken furniture and other trash were blanketed with cobwebs and dust.

Jack figured there was a reason for him to be led there. He started digging through that trash pile. Near the bottom of the pile, Jack found several old leather bags. One was filled with silver coins, one was filled with gold, another held sparkly jewelry, shining like a bag of stars. There were other bags, too, filled with silver cups and tableware and other fine treasures.

Jack stood up and looked at the hand. But it wasn't just a hand anymore. First it was the bony figure that Jack had used to play tenpins, except for that burning hand. Then flesh formed around the bones and clothes wrapped around the flesh, and there stood that man who had fallen down the chimney.

The man glowed like an ember about to burn itself out. He smiled at Jack.

"Young sir," said the glowing man, "I have tried to scare you more than once. But here you are, a brave lad, and you have found my treasure. I hid it here when robbers came, for my wealth was more important to me than my life. I know that was foolish. They killed me, they cut me into pieces and stuffed my body up the chimney. They set a fire to burn me down to bones. They did that because I wouldn't tell them where I'd hidden my valuables, and they never found what I had hidden. I'm dead, but the treasure remains, with no one to inherit it, until now.

"You seem to be a bright and brave young man, someone who will be willing to tend to this house no matter what it might hold, and to stand your ground in the face of fear...."

"But I ain't found the face of fear yet," said Jack. "I just found you."

The glowing man laughed. "No matter," he said. "I have told you my story, and I give you my wealth. And now that I have passed on my legacy, I can rest in peace."

The glowing man began to fade. Jack watched him become a shadow, then a memory. And the cellar was dark again.

Well, the next morning, the farmer from the valley came up to the house on the hill. He expected it to be empty, and he wondered if he should just tear it down. He'd thought about that many times, but he was afraid that whatever had haunted the hill might end up in his valley.

He didn't care about the stories of hidden treasure. He figured they were just rumor and gossip. Yes, if that young man was gone this morning, the sensible thing to do was to give up on reclaiming the property, to tear down the house and sell the land. Still, the farmer brought his pretty young daughter up the hill, just in case Jack was still around.

Jack was. He was sitting on the front steps. He had a leather bag hanging over each shoulder, and a pile of silver coins resting on the porch beside him.

"G'mornin', mister," Jack said with a grin. "I'm still here, and I think I can pay you that cheaper than fair price for this house. Would this bunch of coins cover it?"

The farmer nearly fell over. "Yes!" he smiled. "Why, you brave boy, this will pay for the house and more! You can have the land it's built on. You can have the hill. And, well, I'd like you to meet my daughter."

The farmer's daughter was as pretty as a sunrise herself. Her smile fairly lit up Jack's heart. He grinned the biggest grin he'd ever worn on his young face. "Hi," was all he said.

The farmer's daughter touched Jack's hand. "Daddy's been hopin' to find a feller to be my husband and make this house a home for me. I guess you're that feller. I guess you're gonna be my husband!" Standing on tiptoe, she kissed Jack's cheek.

Suddenly, Jack felt a chill. The hair at the nape of his neck stood on end. Goosebumps popped out all over his arms. His face turned hot and red, but his hands and feet got cold. His toes got all tingly, and his teeth started to chatter. His body began to shiver, then to shake like the tenpin bones in his ghostly game.

Jack jumped off the porch and ran, with the leather bags flapping on either side of him.

"Thank you!" he shouted back toward the farmer and his daughter. "I think I found my fear! Keep the house! I don't want it. And I don't want to git married yet!"

Jack ran back through the woods and onto the road and back to his mama. But he never dropped those leather bags, nor a coin or a cup or a piece of jewelry from inside them.

Jack's mama ended up with treasure that helped her set her house and farm in good order. But the greater treasure was the knowledge that her brave boy, young soldier Jack, had finally found his fear.

STORY NOTES

Daddy called this story "Soldier Jack." He didn't tell it much. But I think he felt a connection to the young soldier. Daddy was a second lieutenant among the last graduating classes of the Tuskegee Airmen; his battle was on American soil, not overseas. He was one of the young men who helped to integrate U.S. troops. Then he came home to his mama.

Soldier Jack might have suffered from post-traumatic stress disorder. His post-war behaviors could've killed him, yet he remained unafraid. That is, unafraid until the possibility of an unwanted marriage reared its head.

The war in this variant of the story is the U.S. Civil War. Fort Sumter in North Carolina was attacked with the firing of fifty cannons by Confederate forces in April, 1861. Many young men lost their lives in the following years. And many of those who returned to their homes on either side of the Mason-Dixon Line were changed, both physically and psychologically, from the boys they had once been. Still, they came home to their mamas, who had also suffered in the war.

Bowling was a nine-pin game until 1841, when the game was banned in Connecticut because it was associated with gambling. To circumvent the law, players added a tenth pin.[1] Daddy referred to Soldier Jack's bowling game as tenpins; Dad said the pins were bottles or candlesticks, or whatever the soldiers could find. In 1862, the wooden bowling ball was invented. Don't ask me why I remember that, or who invented it. I tried finding an answer for you, and I'm still looking. Up until that time, I'm wondering what was used to knock down the pins? Some kids in our neighborhood once tried to bowl using Coke bottles and rocks.

It was a very short game.

Dad's variant of the "Soldier Jack" tale didn't include the magical medicine bottle that, when filled with spring water, allows Jack to see Death, or the miraculous sack in which Death can be caught. These are important props in the version called "Whickety-Whack, Into My Sack" as told by the beloved Appalachian storyteller Ray Hicks and preserved in the anthology *QPB Treasury of North American Folktales*[2]. You can also find that story as "Soldier Jack" in Richard Chase's *The Jack Tales*[3].

1. Visit—History of Bowling. http://www.bowlingmuseum.com/Visit/HistoryofBowling.aspx

2. Catherine Peck, editor. *QPB Treasury of North American Folktales* (New York: Quality Paperback Book Club, 1998).

3. Richard Chase. *The Jack Tales.* (Boston: Houghton, 1943).

Siftin' Sand

A farmer had a field that he wanted to plant with taters, so he could make a little more money. But the field had lain fallow for a long time. It was covered with rocks and overgrown with weeds and the soil needed turning, aerating, fertilizing, what folks called "sifting".

The farmer had only one young son to help with all the work, so he tried to hire somebody to get that late-season planting done. He sent word into town that whoever came to work that field for him would have plenty to eat, and would stay in the cabin that was fenced in at the middle of the field.

But if somebody came to help work that field in the daytime, they were gone by evening. If they came in the evening, they never stayed until midnight. For that cabin and the whole field around it were haunted.

If just the hint of the shadow of a cloud fell on that field, something would rise in the shadow and walk toward the fence, come through the gate, and walk right into the cabin. So nobody stayed there. And after a while, nobody came looking for work.

The farmer figured he'd just have to do with the harvest he'd gather from other fields, because he just wasn't going to get the taters planted.

Then early one evening, a young man knocked at the back

door of the farmhouse. He was tall, and thin, and dressed in a brand new pair of blue jeans, and a pair of brown leather work boots with nice, thick soles and brand new laces.

The farmer opened the door, looked the young man up and down. The young man grinned.

"Hey," he said, "my name is Jack Sprat. Well, not really, but folks call me that 'cause I'm so skinny. I come to see if you got some work for me."

"Well, yes," said the farmer, "there is work that needs to be done. There's this field I want to plant with taters. But, well, there's this ... there's this ... ghost ..."

"Aw, say no more about that," said Jack Sprat. "I heard all about yer ghost in town, and I ain't afraid of anything like that. I ain't afraid of anything!

"So, if you give me a bite to eat and a place to spend the night, I'll be ready to work that field for you come mornin'."

Well, the farmer and his young son took Jack down to the cabin. They walked him across the field and through the back gate. They took him through the cabin and settled him into the old rocking chair on the front porch. They lit the lamp in the front room and the cook-stove in the kitchen, brought Jack a cast iron skillet and some fatback to grease it, and a small sack of taters from the last harvest on another field. The farmer sharpened Jack's knife so he could peel and slice those taters, and brought him some tobacco for his pipe. With the lamp and stove lit and Jack settled in, rocking in the rocking chair, peeling and slicing taters into his hat, puffing on his pipe there on the front porch, the farmer and his son went on back home.

Jack sat there, rocking and peeling and slicing, puffing on his pipe, and everything was just fine. Until the sun went down.

From the far corner of the field, Jack heard something. It was a voice, singing to him:

"I'm comin' 'cross the field, siftin' sand, *coulee*-coo ..."

Jack told himself, it's the wind. It's just the wind. He kept on peeling and slicing those taters, rocking in that rocking chair, and puffing on his pipe.

From about midway between the edge of the field and the fence's front gate, Jack heard again

"I'm comin' 'cross the field, siftin' sand, coulee-coo...."

Jack stopped rocking. He listened, but he didn't hear anything more. And just in case it was the farmer's son trying to scare him, Jack sang back,

"Well, I'm sittin' on the front porch peelin' the taters, cooey-coo!"

And he went on rocking, peeling and slicing, puffing on his pipe ...

From someplace near the fence, Jack heard:

"I'm standin' at the front gate, siftin' sand, coulee-coo...."

Jack stopped rocking again. He dropped his pipe. He took a deep breath. "It's gittin' kinda cold out here," he said. "I think I'll go inside."

Jack gathered up everything on the front porch and headed for the front door of that cabin. But, just in case it *was* the farmer's son playing tricks on him, Jack sang out,

"I'm headin' for the front door, totin' the taters, cooey-coo!"

Jack walked on in the cabin. The lamp was still lit in the front room, and the skillet on the cookstove was hot. Jack put that fatback in the skillet. It started snapping and crackling and popping, made the whole cabin smell like bacon.

A voice sang,

"I'm comin' through the front gate, smellin' the fatback, coulee-coo ...."

Jack sang back,

"Well, I'm standin' in the kitchen, greasin' the skillet, cooey-coo!"

Jack threw those sliced taters into the skillet. Good gracious, that stuff smelled good!

That voice sang, "I'm headin' for the front door, smellin' the taters, coulee-coo!"

And right then, that lamp in the front room ... went ... OUT!

Jack sang back, "I'm headin' for the back door, quick as I can, cooey-coo!"

Jack started trotting to the back door.

The voice sang, "I'm comin' in the kitchen, smellin' the taters, coulee-coo ...."

Jack sang back, "Well, I'm runnin' for the back steps, quick as I can, cooey-coo!"

The voice sang, "I'm heading for the back steps, quick as I can, coulee-coo ...."

Jack sang back, "I'm runnin' for the back gate, quick as I can, cooey-coo!"

The voice sang, "I'm ... right *behind* ya ... 'bout ta *get* ya ... siftin' *sand* ... coulee ... cooooo ... GOTCHA!"

The next morning, before sunrise, that farmer got up from his night's sleep and looked out the bedroom window. He saw smoke rising from the chimney hole for that cookstove, and he smelled fatback and taters. So he figured Jack had done alright for himself.

The farmer woke up his son and they went down to the cabin to help Jack do some work. But when they got to the back gate, lying on the ground just inside that gate was a pair of brand new blue jeans, and a pair of brown leather work boots with nice, thick soles and brand new laces ... and nobody in them.

The farmer said, "Hmmm, I wonder what happened to Jack Sprat."

His young son said, "Daddy, I don't care what happened to Jack Sprat. Sun ain't up all the way. There's shadows on this field. I'm wonderin' w-w-where ... that ... *ghost* is!"

And a voice from the cabin's kitchen sang,

"I'm standin' in the kitchen, eatin' the taters, *sprinkled with JACK SPRAT …*

Sho' taste GOOOOD! … ha, ha, ha, ha …"

℘ ℘

STORY NOTES

That's where the story ended. Right after the farmer and his son discovered the sharecropper's empty boots! In that agrarian economy, nobody would leave a good pair of boots behind, which meant that Jack had met a bad end. If there was any doubt about it, the voice from within the cabin confirmed Jack's fate when he sang out about eating potatoes "sprinkled with Jack Sprat." At that terrifying moment, my daddy would stop his telling and turn off the light in my room. Daddy would tuck me in, kiss me goodnight, and expect me to go to sleep!

And, I guess, that's as good a place as any to end this chapter.

A Sense of Place and Time
And One Last Story

My great-grandmother, Essie, didn't tell a lot of stories, but she always seemed to have a new one for me when I came to visit. Sometimes she read them with me from the Bible. Sometimes, she showed them to me in old books of fairytales and told me to sit on the front-porch glider and read them. On a few occasions as I grew older, Great-Grandma told me "the news" about people she knew in East Liverpool, Ohio, even if I didn't know the folks about whom she spoke.

Still, there were many stories that were never told.

My great-grandparents, Great-Pop Jerome and Great-Grandma Essie Arkward, were only a short generational step away from the times of Africans' captivity in the United States, yet I never heard their stories of growing up "in the times." They shelved the toughest stories of their youth in some library deep inside themselves. I don't recall ever hearing them speak one word about their childhood experiences and memories. But I do remember occasional shadows of … something … darkening their moods, changing the warmth of their smiles to cool, wistful stares into some world I did not know. This usually happened after they had talked with old friends, visitors or the older men who came to their house for room and board—in those days, hotels were not welcoming to people of color.

The visits would be full of laughter and conversation, but

sometimes, when little ears weren't around, the talk would get serious, and the shadows would pass over the front porch, even on the sunniest days of summer. Then someone would crack a joke, or start to tell or retell some life experience, and the shadows would pass, clouds that had threatened a rain that never came, because it had already passed.

The only time I ever saw one of my great-grandparents cry was after Great-Pop's funeral. He'd died of cancer, but, in his most difficult moments, he had never shed a tear. He died when I was ten years old, too young to completely understand the treasure that I had lost.

People had filled the house, first with whispered reverence, then with stories of what a good man Great-Pop had been. Windows were opened, so Great-pop's soul could leave. Food appeared, in casseroles and roasting pans, cake pans and pie tins; folks hustled and bustled in and out of the kitchen, and children kept being told: "Eat. You eat? Go eat! Good. Now go play."

Eventually, the house grew quieter, people having shared their prayers and regards and blessings of food, and gone back to their own homes. Many of them took pots or plates of food with them, so that Great-Grandma wouldn't have to worry about returning the favor of a meal. The saying was, never return a pot without putting something in it. As neighbors and friends departed, they left behind these words for Great-Grandma: "I'll be by to check on you."

Most of the folks who remained were family, women washing dishes and dividing up or putting away the abundance of leftovers (it was called "funeral food"). There would be a few men and women on the front porch with the preacher, a lot more men on the back porch with my grandfather, Great-pop's son. Ice swirled in glasses and canning jars of tea, or lemonade, or maybe something a bit harder for the men on the back porch, since the preacher was on the front porch. Children chased fireflies around the long front yard, while a few older ones sat on the steps talking in the secretive tones of adolescence.

Great-Grandma had changed from her black dress to her flowered housedress, removed her stockings and put on her mules, and put away her little black, veiled hat. Now she sat in Great-Pop's chair in the living room. I sat on the floor, with my head on her knee. She sat quietly, her hands gently rubbing the worn upholstery where Great-Pop's arms had rested. Then she pulled a handkerchief from the pocket of her housedress, and held it to the corners of her eyes. I remember her touching my head in the same way she touched the arms of that chair. Then she put the hanky back in her pocket, and went into the kitchen to supervise the work. No more tears, no sadness in the kitchen, just the sounds of pots, pans, and conversation. That's what I remember.

I also remember her telling me a short story:

Love and Death

On a sultry summer's day, feeling faint under the noonday sun, that fellow called Cupid sought a respite in the shadows of a cave deep in the woods. At the back of the cave, where the air was nice and cool, rested Death.

Cupid's body felt heavy with sweat and exhaustion. He carelessly tossed his bow and quiver from his shoulders to the ground. His arrows fell from the quiver to the floor of the cave, where they mixed in with the arrows spilled from the quiver of Death.

Death had ambled into that cave in the same condition as Cupid, and done the very same thing with his own bow and arrows. And now, both slept soundly, until a soft breeze whispered, "The sun is setting."

Both those odd fellows rose, and stretched, and barely looked at one another. They gathered arrows for their quivers. Each slung a quiver over his shoulder. Then each took up his bow, and without a word to one another, they left the cave.

Of course, Death now carried some of Cupid's arrows, and Cupid carried some of Death's.

And so it is that elders often feel the pains of love, and, with great sorrow and shock for all who are around them, the young meet Death. And, to this day, death and love both strike without a warning.

✤ ✤

I think Great-Grandma cried a little more then. I know I felt like crying. But I don't remember staying in the kitchen with her.

The next day, the old atmosphere of love, peace, and great joy filled that home in East Liverpool, Ohio. And the stories I heard were joyful ones. The only mention Great-Grandma made of feeling any pain or sadness came in reply to a question I posed, something like, "Great-Grandma, are you gonna be okay, here, by yourself?"

I can't be sure of all her words, but there were a couple sentences I won't forget: "God's with me; your great-grandpa is, too. Life won't be a bed of roses, and it won't be the briar patch."

A briar patch or a bed of roses? To me, both were prickly places, uncomfortable at the least. I wanted to ask Great-Grandma Essie what she meant, but I thought it might not be the time for explanations.

Much later in my own life, I could reason that the bed of roses was supposed to be an easy life. The phrase comes from a poem by English poet Christopher Marlowe (1564–1593), posthumously published in 1599. The poem, "The Passionate Shepherd to His Love," begins with the well-remembered phrase, "Come live with me and be my love ..." and includes this verse:

> "There I will make thee beds of roses
> And a thousand fragrant posies,
> A cap of flowers, and a kirtle
> Embroidered all with leaves of myrtle;"

I guess Marlowe was speaking of rose petals, not the rosebush's vines and thorns. Had I known what the phrase meant when I was ten and Great-pop died, I would have wished for that bed of roses for Great-Grandma.

The briar patch was a troublesome place, thickly tangled and full of thorns. Some folks said that nobody but Brer Rabbit could live in a briar patch. But Daddy said he didn't live there. He was just born there.

"Rabbit started in the briar patch, but he had sense enough to get out of there. And if somebody threw him back in, he found a way to live through it, and get through it, and get out again."

Mama and Daddy showed me the blackberries that grew there, too. I thought all briar patches grew blackberries, something sweet and nourishing among the thorns, something that kept you alive until you could get out. And getting out was a prickly struggle, but it could be done.

Over the years, I have come to understand. Some of us were bred and born in a briar patch. Some of us found shelter there, and we still return to it to nourish the soul. Thanks to its stories, and the sweet nourishment I could glean from them, thanks to all the rabbits who found a home and a way in a thicket of troublesome times. I can respect my roots, and still see, walk, and live beyond the briar patch.

❧❧ ❧❧

Reading Group Extras

❧❧ ❧❧

About the Author

Lynette (Lyn) Ford is a fourth-generation Affrilachian storyteller She is an Ohio teaching artist with the Ohio Alliance for Arts Education (OAAE) and the Ohio State-Based Collaborative Initiative of the Kennedy Center for the Arts (OSBCI). This is her second book of Affrilachian tales. Lyn shares them to honor her elders and ancestors, and to preserve for her children, grandchildren, and extended story-loving family the heritage of orature she has gathered.

Lyn is a member of the Circle of Elders of the National Association of Black Storytellers, and the recipient of a National Storytelling Network Circle of Excellence award. She has performed in the National Storytelling Festival and in residencies for the International Storytelling Center in Jonesborough, Tennessee, as well as for festivals, conferences, and events across the United States and in Ireland. Lyn is a member of the National Storytelling Network, the International Storytelling Network, and several local and regional storytelling organizations.

Lyn's next writing assignment is the perfection of her corn bread recipe ... no sugar added.

Q & A With Author Lyn Ford

Q Why more Affrilachian tales?

A These are my bread and butter, in more ways than one. The tales rooted in my family's orature are both the foundation for my own storytelling as well as the primary stories in most of the programs that I share as a "professional" storyteller.

Q What does the term "orature" mean?

A "Orature" is a term coined by the late Ugandan scholar Pio Zirimu in the early 1970s, as a distinct term for the oral-aural traditions—folk epics, folklore, folksong, proverbs, told bedtime stories, jokes, oral poetry, performance poetry, narrative communicated manually (by voice and/or sign language) … shared without a written medium. Zirimu gave the pre-written roots of story a distinct name and place in narrative history as true literature.

Q Why the title, *Beyond the Briar Patch*?

A There are people, old and young, in urban, agricultural, industrial, and technological regions of this country, who have little to no idea where the tales of "Bugs Bunny" types of trickster/heroes began. There are others who bristle and cringe when they hear the term "briar patch." I'm hoping that people will see this title and be inquisitive enough to open the book. I'm trying to nurture a curiosity about and deeper respect for African American folktales, particularly those of Rabbit, and their roots in African storytelling traditions.

Q Some of the stories in this collection are for children and some are for older readers. Why put them together in one volume of work?

A When I told stories in Ireland a few years ago (at the Cape Clear International Storytelling Festival), one of the moments that gave me the most joy was being in a small room over a pub, where elders sat among younger people, and parents brought their children to sit at their feet and listen to the tellers, no matter what type of tale was being told. If a story was for younger listeners, the adults joined in its interactions with as much energy as the children. If a story was a bit "mature", it sometimes went right over the heads of the little ones, but there were other times when I heard whispers and saw glances between young and old. I knew that the families would talk about the stories, perhaps with some explanations, when they got home.

Ah, I thought, wouldn't it be great to give families the opportunity to share stories from a book in a similar manner? I put the book together with that thought in mind. There are tales for the mature reader, and stories to read to young ones, and the reader can be selective about that. But the book is for the family, across the ages. Reading it can be a shared experience.

Q Although there is a humorous vein throughout the book, you touch on some serious subjects through the inclusion of tales that speak of slavery and war. You tell stories of the slave John and other narratives of American life in the 1800s. What was your reason for including such a serious topic?

A This is an important era of our history. It's not just my history or my family's history or one people's history. It is a major portion of the history of our country, with relevance in today's socio-cultural environment. Again, my reasoning is that stories, even on tough topics, can and should be shared familial experiences. Family should be the safe environment for enlightenment. These experiences can open discussions, encourage conversations and personal research, and give depth and an opportunity for critical thinking on topics that should be more than chapters in school books.

Most of the stories I share have both humor and heart, as well as some connection to history. That's the way I tell. So, that's the way I write.

Q Is telling the stories easier than writing them?

A Yes! I am very much a linguistic and tactile-kinesthetic learner. And I think we work best in a manner that is similar to the way we learn. But I can't use voices and gestures and facial expressions on a piece of paper; the words have to do that. I hope that you'll see the moves of Rabbit or note the exasperation of Jack's mama on a page, just as you might when you see and hear me tell.

So when I translate the stories from orature to literature, my biggest challenge is getting into print format all the energy of characterizations, descriptions and action verbs that I share through physical presentation, pacing, pauses, and nuance. It's a slow and uneasy process, with a lot of revision for "vision", and I talk to myself a lot as I work. But, just like Tortoise competing with the Hare, I don't give up.

Are these stories written exactly as you heard them when you were a child?

 No, they can't be. I remember phrases, rhymes, songs, scenes, and sometimes full paragraphs of stories from my favorite storytellers; I can even hear their voices as I'm telling, which impacts my presentations through voice and gesture at the cell-memory level. But that doesn't mean I have any story memorized word for word, or that I'd dare to say it was exactly what my Daddy said.

I have scenes and actions of characters in my head, but, if they remember a story, my brother and my sister seem to have their own versions of what happened, agreeing only on the protagonists, antagonists, and resolution (most of the time). Funny thing, my grandfather and his cronies were the same way when they told stories … "That's not the way that story goes. Let me tell it. You're killin' it!"

Sometimes I heard the same tale told in several different variants by several different family members. I usually remember my favorite version of the story and my favorite teller.

Q What is your earliest memory of a storytelling experience?

A The earliest memories are of my mother reading to us at bedtime. She'd sit in a chair between our beds in the room I shared with my sister; my brother was already asleep in his crib. Ma read in the light of a small lamp while the clock, shaped like a cat with rolling eyes and a tale that swung back and forth, ticked and tocked away the evening. Ma read with such beauty and imagery that I ran with Black Beauty and walked into the forest with Red Riding Hood.

My favorite storytelling memory is of Daddy putting us all in the bed in the master bedroom on a Saturday night.

We'd all had our baths and smelled like Ivory soap and bleached pajamas. Daddy would lie down in the middle of the bed, with us on both sides of him, and he'd start to tell...something. I would beg for scary stories, but he never started with those; Daddy made up stories, and told versions of folk and fairy tales that nobody else seemed to know. Eventually, my sister and brother would go to sleep, and Daddy would carry them to their own beds. But I'd usually have to walk to mine, because I was determined to hear more stories, and Dad would have to make me go to bed. By that time, I'd heard a good, creepy tale. Then Daddy would tuck me in and kiss me goodnight. And I'd be too scared to sleep!

Q How does the oral tradition stand up to the competition of electronic formats in this era of digital everything?

A Stand up? No, stand out! Storytelling in the oral tradition is a skill that requires more effort and bravery than learning technology. It requires extroverted behavior and a communal connection that electronic networking does not offer, even with the best Skype viewing or shared YouTube narrative. There are folks who would rather die than stand before an audience and speak, yet they can communicate and share a story on the Internet.

I think that is the strength of electronic formats. I also think that storytelling in the oral tradition and digital storytelling can complement one another. Artistic, creative narrative is the key for both of them. I believe there is room for story in any style and format in which it can be shared.

Q You've said that many of your personal resources, people like your father and grandfather, are gone. Let's say you remember only a part of a story. How can you develop partially-remembered stories for presentation?

A When some of a story is missing, I do a lot of research, including asking questions of storytellers who may remember similar stories. I recognize this possibility by experiencing the repertoires of as many tellers as I can. Storytellers are generous folks. We exchange stories, as well as bits of stories we remember. This gives me the opportunity to put the pieces of a story puzzle back together, or to create pieces to fill in where there is an empty space.

After reaping whatever is in my memory, and listening to others and asking a lot of questions, I look for printed formats of the stories in the oldest versions that I can find at university, folklore, and historical libraries. I try to find at least three literary sources, but only after talking with and listening to many, many storytellers, several of whom are members of the National Association of Black Storytellers, whose annual conference has become a family reunion for me.

The personal connection jogs my memory and fills in gaps for me in ways that a printed story can't. And the finished product may not be Daddy's version or Pop-pop's version, but it's a narrative that is as close as my heart can make it.

Q Are you working on another book?

A Yeah, I'm actually working on two! One is a book of original creepy stories, twisted from folk and fairytales, with connections to their motifs and variants. The other is a few more Affrilachian tales, but it's also a collection of folktale variants from the African, Native American, and European oral traditions that are probably the roots of the narratives.

I'm also doing research on the folklore of my family, foods and herbal lore and belief systems that over-arch our own African, Native American, and European heritage. I don't know that all that stuff will be in a book, but the research will enrich my knowledge base, my writing, and my life.

The research for these manuscripts makes the process a lot slower for me, but I love the challenge. It's not a race to publication. I'm more like Tortoise than Hare in my progression. But I also have Tortoise's tenacity.

Slow and steady ...

Author's Comments on the Origins of This Book

I was sitting in the passenger seat of our family car. Bruce—my husband, my partner in life, and my roadie—was driving. I can't remember where we were going, a storytelling program somewhere near Steubenville, I think. But I know we were on the highway next to the Ohio River, Route 7, a road that leads to the spot where three states—Ohio, Pennsylvania, and West Virginia—meet.

East Liverpool breathed memories in my direction, memories of childhood days spent with my great-grandparents, Jerome and Essie Arkward, who were only a few generational steps away from the times of African captivity and slavery in the United States. Dim remembrances of the bridge from Ohio to Chester, West Virginia, called up visions of rich green hills and valleys, stories of pottery works, coal mines and the dirty railways that attend coal mines. The childhood memories also included painful memories of social ostracism during the 1960s of my youth. Physical memories and social memories ran together, like the mountain streams of that area. Obstructions constructed by the prejudices of the times—from the Civil War to the '60s, and even to current events—were palpable on that day.

Visible through foliage as we sped along, the river ran low but rapidly. I thought of how I'd been told that, in the 1800s, there were times when the Ohio River was so low that runaway folks could actually wade its width from Kentucky and what was then Virginia,* to seek freedom in Ohio. The old spiritual played in my sub-conscious,

wade in the water, wade in the river ....

These memories were clear, but, in some ways, my mind was as foggy as the lowest stretches of the highway. Along that stretch of road and river lay stories not yet told, stories of Affrilachian kith and kin, hidden histories touched by and touching the river, legends and lore left unspoken, a culture's treasures left behind in the place where Ohio, Pennsylvania, and West Virginia meet.

That cultural treasure is the heritage and traditions of Affrilachians.

Although I've shared a collection of Affrilachian folktales and lore, I know there is much that can still be shared. Stories are waiting for the story-catchers and the story-keepers to draw them from the waters or to pluck them from the leaves and the voices of the Appalachian region. This second book does not gather all of them, but it presents some important ones from my heritage that did not come to mind when I was working on my first book. And, God willing, I am still blessed with a little time, a few storytelling friends who share the same African American Appalachian roots, and a lot of memories. With their cheerful sense of community, and the blessing of continued health, I will do what I can.

The stories are not forgotten. Like tobacco and cotton crops of old, they wait for harvesting. Some may stain the hands of the reaper; some may come with painful thorns of remembering. But they need us to gather them, and honor them, and tell them, again, and again, and again. Thus, I share a second book of Affrilachian folklore and love with you.

ஒ ௮

*West Virginia became a state during the Civil War, as a result of separation from the secessionist state of Virginia. This separation, which began in 1861 with the western region of Virginia politically splitting away from the eastern region, was formalized when West Virginia was admitted to the Union.

Glossary

Aesopic—pertaining to, or characteristic of Aesop or his fables: a story that points an Aesopian moral

Clabbered—thickened or curdled

Corn cake—There has been debate among old-school cornbread aficionados as to whether adding sugar to the recipe turns a corn bread into a corn cake. Most cornbread recipes today include sugar…look at the ingredients on that box of Jiffy Mix™ before you use it to make corn muffins. Jiffy Mix™ is a trademarked name for a product of the Chelsea Milling Company. For some delightful recipes, go to www.jiffymix.com/recipe.php/. My husband adds an extra egg to the mix, and a little extra milk, and greases the cake pan with bacon grease, and serves the baked delight with ham-and-bean soup. This is my favorite meal on a cool autumn day.

Coulee—a ravine, a dry gulch; the word originated from a Latin word, colare, which means "to sift or purify." (Three years of Latin occasionally prove themselves to have been a handy investment of my time.)

Cushions—Do I really need to explain that? It refers to a part of the anatomy that my mother wouldn't let us easily refer to in our house. We could say "bottom"—her preference—or "behind", but we couldn't say butt, or backside, and definitely not the three-letter word that begins with "a." Daddy and Mama also referred to it as a "tuchus" (Yiddish, from a neighbor lady, but Daddy pronounced it "too´-kus"). When he was getting really perturbed with us and wanted us to stop our over-active antics or arguments and keep still, Daddy called the region an "asquasettus" (pronounced "ā-skwa-set´-us"). We didn't know whether to laugh, or sit, or say, "Yes, sir." Most of the time, we did all three.

Fatback—the hard fat from under the skin of a pig's back, used to make cracklin (pork rinds), some sausages, slab bacon, and lard. A somewhat meatier version of salt pork is called "Streak o'Lean". Once a cast iron skillet was greased and hot, the peeled and sliced "taters" were spread in layers, salted and peppered, covered for a while, then uncovered and turned once as they cooked to a golden color.

Fritter—a fried-batter snack or side dish, usually made with fresh or canned corn and served with hot sauce at suppertime. Our family enjoyed fritters with syrup and butter at breakfast. The batter was rich with eggs and the flavor of bacon grease. The batter was dropped by tablespoons into hot oil in a heavy skillet, turned once, cooked until golden brown and drained on paper towels. This is definitely not something I put on the family menu in this health-conscious century, but the memory of eating them as a child still makes my mouth water to the point of drooling like Fox. And if somebody makes some, well...

Gumption—is one of those words rooted in the Scots-Appalachian heritage shared by folks who might also be children of Africa or the Americas. It means "spunk," nerve, or assertive energy.

Holler—a hollow, ravine or valley

Kente cloth—known as nwentoma in Akan, is a type of silk and cotton fabric made of interwoven cloth strips. An icon of African cultural heritage around the world, Kente cloth has its origins in the Ashanti Kingdom in Western Africa.

Kirtle—a long gown or dress worn by women

Malian bogolanfini—is a hand-made cotton fabric traditionally dyed with fermented mud. Origins are with the Bamana peoples of Mali, West Africa.

Manumission papers—Called "freedom papers," these were the legal documents that ended a term of captivity and set a former slave free in the days before Emancipation.

Moaned—In the story, "The Handsomest Man in the World", moaning is not a dialectic misspelling of the word "mourn." The moan is a sound of grief, beautifully and deliberately created as a hum in minor key; as emotions rise at a funeral service, the moan becomes a wordless song, often punctuated by shouts and cries, collectively shared by the congregation.

Orature— "... the use of utterance as an aesthetic means of expression." ("Notes Towards a Performance Theory of Orature", http://www.ohio.edu/people/hartleyg/ref/Ngugi_Orature.html)

Passel—a large amount; several. In our family, there was a passel, a heap, a mess, and a slew; you'll find "slew" in "Papa Turtle and Monkey" a few pages after this.

Perambulation—This term is introduced by Papa Turtle in "Papa Turtle and Monkey", where Monkey finds out that it means a walk. Monkey was a bit perturbed to find out that it might even mean a lo-o-ong walk.

Piddlin'—is a very descriptive word, indicating that an amount is unbelievably and pitifully trivial.

Simenjous—Pop-pop's word for bigger than big, or enormous. He knew which adjectives meant "big", but he was very good at making up his own descriptive words.

Slew—a large amount. This word is rooted in the Irish influence on language in Appalachia.

Slumgullion—a watery stew made with potatoes or noodles, mixed vegetables, and whatever meat was available. The word is very old, from at least the 1800s, as stated at "World Wide Words", www.worldwidewords.org/ and at Merriam-Webster Online, www.merriam-webster.com.

Sufficiently seransifyin': a term that grew from my daddy saying he was "sufficiently seransified" when his palate was happy, his stomach was full, and his plate was empty. I felt like "Pig's Nose" was the story in which I could introduce that wonderfully descriptive phrase.

Wampus—meanness.

Wampus cat—a fearsome creature of Appalachian folklore, half woman, half wild cat.

Her roots are in her culture and stories

"A rich and unique landscape peopled with characters and plots as unusual as they are delightful."

—**Jim May**, Storyteller, Author and Educator, IL

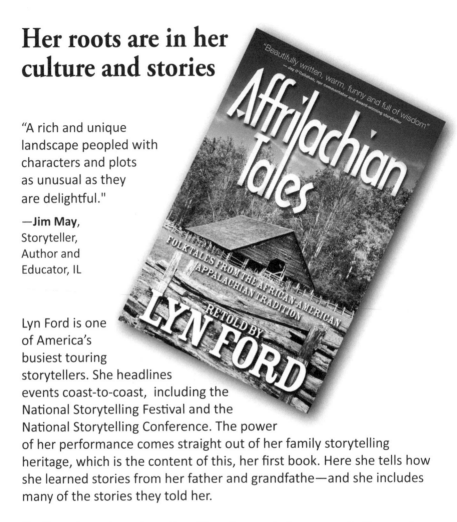

"Beautifully written, warm, funny and full of wisdom"
— Jay O'Callahan, npr commentator and award-winning storyteller

Affrilachian Tales

FOLKTALES FROM THE AFRICAN AMERICAN APPALACHIAN TRADITION

RETOLD BY **LYN FORD**

Lyn Ford is one of America's busiest touring storytellers. She headlines events coast-to-coast, including the National Storytelling Festival and the National Storytelling Conference. The power of her performance comes straight out of her family storytelling heritage, which is the content of this, her first book. Here she tells how she learned stories from her father and grandfathe—and she includes many of the stories they told her.

"... The minute I read the line, 'One does not give power to those who try to subvert knowledge, simply because it does not fit into their own worldview,' I knew that I was going to love this book. And that was just the preface."
—**Kim Weitkamp**, Humorist and Storyteller, West Virginia

PARKHURST BROTHERS PUBLISHERS

Paperback · ISBN 978-1-935166-66-5
160 Pages @ 6" x 9"
Ebook · eISBN 978-1-935166-67-2
www.parkhurstbrothers.com

For more books about the oral storytelling tradition,
we invite you to visit
www.parkhurstbrothers.com
and to visit our Facebook page:
Facebook/Parkhurst Brothers Publishers